PREACHING
WITH A
Problem

PREACHING
WITH A
Problem

A GUIDEBOOK FOR RELIGIOUS LEADERS

DR. AARON MCNAIR SR.

iUniverse LLC
Bloomington

Preaching with a Problem
A Guidebook for Religious Leaders

iUniverse books may be ordered through booksellers or by contacting:

iUniverse LLC
1663 Liberty Drive
Bloomington, IN 47403
www.iuniverse.com
1-800-Authors (1-800-288-4677)

Because of the dynamic nature of the Internet, any web addresses or links contained in this book may have changed since publication and may no longer be valid. The views expressed in this work are solely those of the author and do not necessarily reflect the views of the publisher, and the publisher hereby disclaims any responsibility for them.

Any people depicted in stock imagery provided by Thinkstock are models, and such images are being used for illustrative purposes only.
Certain stock imagery © Thinkstock.

ISBN: 978-1-4759-9255-7 (sc)
ISBN: 978-1-4759-9257-1 (hc)
ISBN: 978-1-4759-9256-4 (ebk)

Printed in the United States of America

iUniverse rev. date: 07/05/2013

CONTENTS

CONTENTS

DEDICATION

My Mother Betty McNair   My Sister Doris Ellis

This book I dedicated to my precious mother, "Betty McNair" whom peacefully closed her eyes on January 7, 2013 and went home to be with the Lord. I will be forever grateful to her for all that she has ever meant to me, her untiring support and encouragement. She will be forever loved and forever missed.

Also this book is dedicated to my darling sister, Doris Lorraine Ellis.

Our family affectionately called her Rain.

She went home to be with the Lord on May 23, 2012. I will forever be grateful for a sister who always supported me and was very proud of me.

She will live in my heart forever.

FOREWORD
BY APOSTLE VONNER G. HORTON

Apostle McNair has captured every preacher's testimony in this book Preaching with a Problem. As he makes it crystal clear through sermons and wisdom birthed out of experience that the call on the life of the preacher is a permanent call. It is indeed a call from God without repentance. It is clearly seen in this book that as the Apostle Paul was given a thorn in his flesh and even after repeatedly asking God to remove the thorn, God's decision was to not remove the thorn but rather to give Paul His grace to be able to continue ministry with the thorn. Apostle McNair makes it clear that the Good News of the Gospel is far greater than the thorns of the preacher and nothing that life throws our way is to move us away from our divine assignment. We are supposed to function with our thorns. He reminds us that every Christian must experience the pain and joy of their God given assignment.

However this book is not only for the preacher but also for every member that sits in the pew as he teaches the parishioners that God has given a dual responsibility. The first responsibility is given to the preacher (shepherd) to care for the sheep and then to the followers too care for the shepherd. Often time the pew members forget their responsibility to their Shepherds. He deals with Aaron and Hur taking their places on the left and right side of Moses to keep their leader's arms lifted in the time of battle to guarantee victory. By this he reminds every pew member that they have the responsibility to keep their leaders arms lifted up. Apostle McNair in one chapter asks a question to the pew members, "Who cares if you die?" with a strong focus on the value of the leader in the life of the pew members.

One of the chapters that will really grasp the heart of every leader is titled Leading with Integrity. Here the writer stresses the need of integrity in the life of the leaders. He makes it clear that integrity is our security. In an addition, Apostle McNair teaches that we must "Go the Full Measure" in the face all pressures, trials, sicknesses, afflictions, and struggles, we are yet called to go all the way for Christ. We cannot stop at any point because of the magnitude of our troubles. How well do I know this from my own times of struggles, sufferings and losses. In the genesis of my pastorate I was a Bi-vocational pastor working in the public school system in the classroom then advancing to the administrative offices. The problem was the ministry was a full time job and the school was a full time job but I was only one person doing the work of two people. It was hard bearing the burden of doing what was necessary to care for my daughter and home while knowing that God would not allow me to be slack in ministry. The preacher must continue in spite of his or her own thorns. I came to realize this while experiencing my marriage falling apart and having to counseling others to keep their homes together. Seminary doesn't teach the preacher how not to loose yours while saving everyone else. Functioning as a single parent, dealing with a failed marriage, and facing all of the issues that befalls any pastor, I must say that my most traumatic experience was the sudden death of my strongest supporter, my confidant and my prayer partner—my beloved mother. It is at this point in my life that I realized that no matter how anointed you are or how great the call is on ones life it doesn't make us impervious to the pain and reality of the death of a loved one. I felt like my life had lost purpose and my world had crumbled all around me. Questioned raged within me that I couldn't blurt out to those I had preached to. I was dealing with the feeling of being let down by God because I asked him to return her to me and He chose not to. Living with immeasurable pain and facing the fact that after the funeral there would be a congregation of people sitting and waiting to be fed like a baby chick with its mouth helplessly open waiting on the mother bird to feed it. Talk about preaching with a problem I returned to the pulpit not healed but remembering the call and the assignment. Apostle McNair makes it clear that Paul's thorn in his flesh was not defined however one of my thorns was clearly defined in February 1991 to me through a medical diagnosis, cancer. For 21 years I have battled cancer telling my self that I have it but it does not have me neither does it define me. I have repeatedly told myself that this sickness is not unto death. Proving to the devil and myself in 1997 after I was announced clinically dead but God brought me back to life. Although I could not understand why I couldn't get a clean bill of health and one day while I was at the Hampton Minister's Conference Bishop Noel Jones walked pass me then suddenly stopped and came back to me and said, "The Lord told me to tell you not to try to get rid of your affliction because it is attached to your anointing and assignment." Bishop Jones' statement to me is reflected in Apostle McNair's book as he teaches that God may not ever take away the thorn but He will surely give us the grace to function with it.

I realize as Apostle McNair teaches, that through it all I must embrace my assignment as my afflictions embraced me and continue.

This book enlightens us that we must **Work Before Harvest Time** without getting weary in well doing and without fainting along the way. This book teaches us that we don't quit! Our shared testimony is that we have been through enough to make us cry, we've been through enough to make us holler, we've been through enough to make us frustrated, we've been through enough to make us fall on our faces, but we haven't been through enough neither shall we ever go through enough to make us quit! We must preach (function) with our problems.

To read more of my personal story read my books: The first one is titled: 50 Motivational & Empowering Quotes to Heal the Broken Woman and the second book is titled: On Broken Pieces

Apostle Vonner G. Horton
New Oxley Hill Baptist Church
Merry Hill, NC
www.newoxleyhillbaptistchurch.com

INSPIRATIONAL EPIGRAPH

"We've got some difficult days ahead, but it really doesn't matter to me now . . .

Because I've been to the mountaintop. And I don't mind. Like anybody I would like to live a long life. Longevity has its place. But I'm not concerned about that now. I just want to do God's will. And He's allowed me to go up to the mountain. And I've looked over. And I've seen the Promise Land. So I'm happy tonight. I'm not worried about anything. I'm not fearing any man. Mine eyes have seen The glory of the coming of the Lord."

—Martin Luther King Jr.,

God of our life, there are days when the burdens we carry chafe our shoulders and weigh us down; when the road seems dreary and endless, the skies grey and threatening; when our lives have no music in them, and our hearts are lonely, and our souls have lost their courage. Flood the path with light, run our eyes to where the skies are full of promise; tune our hearts to brave music; give us the sense of comradeship with heroes and saints of every age; and so quicken our spirits that we may be able to encourage the souls of all who journey with us on the road of life, to Your honor and glory.

—Augstine

Dr. Aaron McNair Sr.

> *In this crazy world, there's an enormous distinction between good times and bad, between sorrow and joy. But in the eyes of God, they're never separated. Where there is pain, there is healing. Where there is mourning, there is dancing. Where there is poverty, there is the kingdom.*
>
> —Henri J. M. Nouwen

Nouwen Centre

One of the great tasks of the preacher is to deal honestly and faithfully with the issues of pain, suffering, and problems. Jesus did. He was clear in this world you will have tribulations and problems. Sometimes not because of the lack of faith but because of the way the faithful must walk in a resistant world. Jesus pulls no punches on problems and neither can we if we are to be faithful to a gospel that bids us to bear a cross. Theodicy that wrestles with the why and hows of life in the midst of life struggles in a theoretical task that cannot and should not be taken lightly. The preacher must face his or her own problems, his or her own faith, and frailty even as he or she stands to proclaim, teach, and help those whom God allows them to declare a word of faith to. Faith does come by hearing but often the hearing must drill through and penetrate problems that seek to block hearing. Pain and problems can be unexpected, uncharted, and unforgiving and yet we declare a word and a hope that we do have to live as though we are able to face them as long as the unconditional love and unstoppable power of God through Jesus Christ is available. Apostle McNair has taken on the task of faithfully facing the problem of problems in his preached and written word. Hear ye what the Spirit says through him.

Rev. Dr. William Barber II
Pastor—Greenleaf Christian Church
(Disciples of Christ)
State Conference President NC NAACP

PREFACE

My Story

In 1993, while living a life that was calm and progressive, my wife Michelle, our son Aaron Jr., and I moved out of Fayetteville, North Carolina, and began living in Florence, South Carolina. Shortly after moving to South Carolina our daughter Jaquetta was born. During the week I was employed with the Florence County Schools and Perdue Farms; I also traveled from state to state every weekend as an evangelist. Michelle worked as a nurse's assistant at the Commander Nursing Center while little Junior attended elementary school and Jaquetta was just learning to crawl. Life wasn't bad as we were preparing to buy our first house in Florence. Then one day the phone rang, and on the other end was my uncle and pastor, Dr. Howard E. McNair Sr., who was serving our denomination as a district elder, assisting the bishops in filling vacant pulpits. He asked me to come back to Goldsboro for a meeting.

When I arrived for the meeting, I met with two lifelong members of the New Mt. Moriah Church, which was affiliated with the United Holy Church International. They expressed their interest in having me become the next pastor of their church. Michelle and I were asked to attend a second meeting with the executive board of the church. After a brief interview, they asked me to come back and preach in the fall of 1995. The first message I preached was "The Hand of God."

After that, I had another interview to talk about moving to Farmville, North Carolina, to be their pastor. It all seemed to be moving too fast, so Michelle and I began praying to ensure that this move was indeed the will of God. In September of 1995 I officially became this church's pastor. Here in my office where I'm typing this, I can see the signatures of the late Bishop H. W. Fields and Dr. Margaret B. Parker affixed to my Certificate of Appointment. My Credentials of Ordination, dated September 25, 1994, also bears those names as well as those of many other great preachers, many of whom have since fallen asleep: Elder E. L. Lawson (deceased), Dr. Ollie G. Harris, Elder John H. Bradley III, Elder Howard E. McNair, Elder Norman E. Johnson Jr. (deceased), Elder Rufus McAllister (deceased), Elder Charles Dingles, Elder Harry Cohen, Elder Sidney Harris, and Elder Gladys Surles. And so the journey began.

My Arrival in Farmville

The church building, about two and a half years old, was a beautiful edifice located off the main street in the small town of Farmville. It sat directly across from a large housing project, and because it was so close to this housing project, I knew that with a little prayer and evangelism we could grow swiftly and impact the community with an effective ministry. I had been told about a lot of good opportunities by the executive board members, but after I officially became the pastor, I learned other details that had been left out of both meetings.

Among many:

- The church was still in litigation with its former pastor and a group of people who had split from my new congregation.
- The church was not financially stable, and the bank had considered foreclosing but didn't want to create bad public relations in this small town.
- The state's appellate court was considering action that would close the church, which kept many former members

away from the church and kept new people from coming to join the church.

- The church was known as a troubled church.
- Most of the members did not fully trust another pastor and had no trouble expressing it.
- Many members were wounded and emotionally scarred and could not move past their painful experience of the split; they expected the past to repeat itself.

I began as the official pastor in October 1995 and quickly learned that there was a huge difference between evangelistic preaching and pastoral preaching. As an evangelistic preacher, I traveled around to share soul-stirring messages of encouragement. However, as a pastor, like the apostle Paul, I suddenly found myself having to preach messages to set the house in order. Like Paul, I had to stand with the weight of a divided, disgruntled, and controlling group of people on my heart. As Paul said, "He carried the burden of the churches on his heart." While trying to preach messages of faith and encouragement, I knew that they also needed messages of correction and rebuke. I truly felt like all things would be better once the church was cleared through the courts, but even after we got a call from the church lawyer and were informed that the final judgment was in our favor, many of the people's attitudes remained the same.

We managed to move forward with many successful projects while dealing with people whose mind-sets just would not change.

I come from a family of preachers and pastors; my father, the late Dr. Abner B. Alford, pastored in the Church of Christ in Miami, Florida; my uncle, Dr. Howard E. McNair Sr., was pastor of the New Stoney Hill Church in Goldsboro; my grandfather, the late Odis B. Alford, was pastor of the Church of Christ in Newark, New Jersey; and my grandfather, the late Rev. Arthur D. Walls, was pastor of the Free Hope Baptist Church in Bladensburg, Maryland. Along with many cousins and aunts, my life has been surrounded by a quorum of preachers, but I can honestly say that nothing, no one, no workshop, no seminary can fully prepare a preacher for the experiences he or she will have in pastoral ministry.

During my first year of pastoring, I was approached by three men from the church, cautioning me about their wives; each one came to me on a separate Sunday morning, not caring that after their rude visitations I had to stand before my congregation and try to preach over their slap in the face and attack on my character. Oh, and let me not fail to mention that these women were old enough to be my mother (and grandmother).

Furious, I called my pastor; he listened as, frustrated and yelling, I blew off much steam, and then he simply said to me, "Son, those people have been through a lot. Yes, their judgment is way off, and this is not the end. It will get even worse, but you must pull it together, leave all of this in your office, and go out there and preach."

Wow! Pull it together and go out there and preach. Those were the words of instruction from my pastor, and I've been following them ever since that day. Pull it together and preach with your problem!

I learned that what I heard the old preachers say was nothing less than the truth: "Before your ministry is over, at your best, you will be accused of everything a preacher can be accused of." Bishop Samuel D. Clemmons once said to me while standing in front of the Branch Memorial Tabernacle, "Aaron, whatever folk say about you, don't ever let them be able to say that you're not a preacher. My son, that is the worst charge a preacher can have." He then patted me on the shoulder and said, "Just keep your nose clean and preach."

Now don't get me wrong; like every other pastor, I also have some self-inflicted wounds. I made all the administrative mistakes that a twenty-five-year-old preacher would make while trying to feel his way through this experience called pastoring.

Preaching (functioning) with a problem stood out in my mind, and as I studied the Word of God, I saw that it was the plight of many biblical leaders such as Jonah, Abraham, David, Noah, Jeremiah, Ezekiel, Hosea, Elijah, Joseph, John, and Timothy, not leaving out the apostle Paul. I began preaching to other pastors and encouraging them to do likewise: "Pull it together and preach with your problem."

This particular message has been requested and recommended by many pastors around the world. It has also been published in *The Oxford Book of Sermons.*

No book can hold all the horrific stories of every pastor, but I wanted to share a few of my experiences along with the messages that I have preached; as David said (concerning himself), "I encouraged myself through these tough times in ministry." (1 Samuel 30:6)

ACKNOWLEDGMENTS

First, I would to thank my wife, Michelle McNair, for her love and committed support, for understanding when no one else does, and for encouraging me to move forward in my desire to write this book. Next, I want to thank my children, Aaron Jr., Courtney, and Jaquetta. Their smiles show their love and admiration for their father. Also, I want to thank my mother, Betty, who taught me that Sunday was not a leisure day but a day of worship. To my grandmother, Marie Parker, who always reminds me to be real for Jesus and who sits by the radio every Sunday, waiting to hear my radio broadcast and who lovingly lets me know when I air the same message twice. To all of my sisters—Sharon, Doris, Chanquie, Bessie, and Claudia (and her husband, Clarence Oliver)—who love me enough to drive hundreds of miles to hear me preach one gospel message and then drive back home. To my Aunt Veda, who has always stood by me in support and has lifted me up in prayer. She has been there for spiritual and non-spiritual counseling.

I would also like to thank my mother-in-law and father-in-law for their support. I would like to thank my beloved pastor, Dr. Howard E. McNair Sr., the pastor of the New Stoney Hill United Holy Church in Goldsboro, North Carolina. I will always consider him to be the preacher of preachers. He has taught me by example that the preacher must remain faithful to the preaching of the gospel. When everything looks like it is headed backward, downhill, and in turmoil, his instructions are, "Just keep on preaching!"

I remember my grandmother, the late Voncile Alford, who spent many Sunday evenings in the basement, listening to my cousin Odis and me repeat my grandfather's morning sermons. Two of the most influential preachers in my life are my grandfather, the late Odis B. Alford, and my father, the late Dr. Abner B. Alford.

Last, but far from least, I want to thank the New Mt. Moriah Churches Family, whom I serve as senior pastor; thank you for your love and support for the past years as we labored in the Lord's vineyard together.

Thanks to all for all. If I have forgotten anyone, I'll try to remember you in the next book.

INTRODUCTION

Preaching with a Problem

The endurance (mental and physical stamina) of today's preacher is challenged by the responsibility of the call itself, which carries strenuous responsibilities. In addition to the regular and on-call hours, the mental and physical exertion is like that of no other occupation. The bi-vocational preacher will surely have problems when it comes to study times and sermon preparation time. Yet the preacher must study, and the preacher must preach.

All Eyes on the Preacher: The Problem with Being in the Public Eye

The eyes of scrutiny from family members, parishioners, media, other religious leaders, as well as your own colleagues in the ministry, can become somewhat overwhelming and discouraging, particularly when what they see is almost always far from what you're presenting.

People Problems

Many times in the life of the preacher, particularly the pastor preacher, the negatives begin to far outweigh the positives. Those we try to lead as their pastor often begin to follow the behavior of the children of Israel, when Moses tried to lead them to a place they did not want to go. The agony and stress of hearing without doubt the voice of God, while he gives clear direction for his people, and then watching the people become their own stumbling blocks, keeping them from their own promised land, is a major problem in the life of many pastor preachers.

The Problem of Carrying the Load

Some problems we encounter in our ministries are our own fault. The micromanager preacher tries to do it all himself or herself, and then he or she looks up one day and is on the edge of a breakdown due to maximum overload. Many times we try to do it all ourselves because we refuse to trust others with responsibilities or we previously trusted the wrong ones, who had an Absalom spirit and caused division or problems in the ministry. We must learn through prayer to trust again, remembering to delegate but regulate. Many of us seasoned preachers can honestly say that at one time of our ministry, we were overloaded (and in some areas, we still are). This is also a major problem in the life of the preacher. We need to understand that Acts 6:1-7 ("Select seven men who are well respected and are full of the Spirit and wisdom") was a relief for the apostles as well as for the people. The seven appointed men relieved the pressure of carrying the load from the apostles.

The Problem with Finding Quality Family Time

For preachers who have been blessed with a spouse and children, quality family time is hard to find. They live with the constant knowledge that they're paying the bills, providing care, ensuring that all of the material things are in place for their spouse and children, yet knowing that their greatest desire is unfulfilled: being a part of their lives and enjoying all of the material things. The demands of the ministry will consume their family time as well as personal time unless they learn how to balance their lives. This is certainly a major problem in the lives of many preachers.

The Problems with Traditions

Denominational restraints (traditional strongholds) cause many problems for preachers who are spirit-led, energetic, free-thinking, contemporary, ambitious, and flowing outside of the norm. Many times preachers are not welcome to flow in the fullness of their ability (anointing) because it breaks the traditional flow of the service or the outcome of the service is more than their superiors want produced from anyone other than themselves. Preaching then becomes mentally and spiritually taxing when they're not free to flow. So the problem with denominational restraints (traditions) is just as Mark 7:13 says: it causes "the word of God to be of no effect."

The Problem with Vision

It is a wonderful thing to receive vision from God for direction of your ministry. The only problem is the provision for the vision; the members of your congregation don't always step up to the plate to help support the vision financially. This can delay achieving the vision, but thank God, slow paying members do not cancel the vision. It can be overwhelming to be patient as well as creative in creating alternate revenue streams for the ministry. Oh, how nice it would be if everyone could catch on to the God given assignments, like the children of Israel did in Exodus 35:20-29 and 36:3-7, and give accordingly. Moses made one offering appeal, and the people of a willing heart began giving without fail. In chapter 36, they had to be restrained from giving because they had given too much. Now that problem is not a problem. When finances are not available to complete projects, it weighs on the preacher's mind at all times.

The Impervious Preacher

Preachers are predestined to encounter negatives throughout their ministry. In light of preachers who fall, quit, or are emotionally distraught, and the dismantling of a morally sound society, we must realize that we have a divine assignment. We are not privileged to walk away from it. In this call we fade away through time. Like the apostle Paul, we do not quit this course. We must finish the course. The only way to finish is to be as impervious as the apostle Paul, Elijah, John, Isaiah, Billy Graham, Kathryn Kuhlman, Bishop G. E. Patterson, Jonathan Edwards, D. J. Moody, Smith Wigglesworth, Charles Spergeon, Kenneth Hagin, E. V. Hill, and John Osteen. They were not influenced by the times and surroundings. Instead they lived to influenced their times and surroundings. Be impervious!

Never Clock Out

The preacher never clocks out. It would be so wonderful if all parishioners understood that their pastor is always on the clock. They do not have the ability to leave the work place from Friday to Monday morning. Preachers almost always have preaching, teaching, administering, finances, and other ministry issues on their mind throughout much of their waking lives. We physically exit the pulpit but we never mentally clock out.

I could go on and on about the many problems that preachers encounter, but I think you have gotten the big picture. The problems are numerous, but the assignment remains the same. Preach on, preachers!

CHAPTER 1

The Assignment of Preaching:
Ezekiel 37:1-10

Let's begin with the Command to Preach. It is vital to understand that preaching is not voluntary. It is not a career choice, nor is it something that Mom or Dad or family members convince you that you ought to be doing. True preachers are sent from God. Romans 10:15 says, "How shall they preach except they are sent?" Now this "sent" does not mean sent by any earthly human, but it refers strictly to the true and living God. Only God can call, appoint, and ordain, and heaven knows only God can anoint a person to preach the gospel. Only God can put in preachers what it takes to be a preacher.

Now let's talk about the preacher and the preaching. The preacher proclaims the gospel, God's saving work through Jesus Christ. The Old Testament mentions several prominent preachers. Noah, who was warned of the impending flood and proclaimed God's ark of safety, was called "a preacher of righteousness." Solomon described himself as a preacher who taught "words of truth." At God's direction, Jonah made a preaching mission to Nineveh, declaring God's judgment and mercy. And just like Jonah, all the prophets of the Old Testament were regarded as preachers, particularly Isaiah, Jeremiah, Amos, and Micah.

In the New Testament, the gospel advanced on the wings of preaching. The zeal generated by Pentecost, coupled with the growing persecution of the young church, led the disciples to preach everywhere in the known world. With a sense of urgency,

Jesus and the apostles preached in homes, by the seaside, on the temple steps, and in the synagogues. Wherever you can get people together, remember there is an urgency to preach.

Jesus connected his ministry with that of the prophets and identified his mission as one of proclaiming deliverance (Luke 4:18-19).

Jesus was under a divine order to spread the gospel by means of preaching (Luke 4:43-44). Phillip, the preaching deacon, "preached the things concerning the kingdom of God and the name of Jesus Christ." In sending out the twelve, Jesus commanded them, "As you go, preach, saying, the kingdom of heaven is at hand." The apostle Paul proudly declared his credentials as one whom God "appointed a preacher and apostle." Virtually all New Testament preaching carries an evangelistic thrust. Paul declared, "It pleased God through the foolishness of preaching that man can be saved."

The distinction between preaching and teaching made in the church today is not evident in the New Testament. Some people today say, "It's time out for preaching and the minister just needs to stick to teaching," but both Jesus and Paul regarded themselves as preachers and teachers. Luke reports that Jesus was appointed "a preacher, an apostle, and a teacher of the Gentiles" (2 Timothy 1:11). The best New Testament preaching, while aimed at motivating sinners to receive Christ, had a strong element of teaching. Paul charged young Timothy to preach the Word! Convince, rebuke, exhort, with all long-suffering and teaching, teach if you have to sometimes, but remember the command is to preach.

Now, when God calls and commands us to preach, we may run like Jonah, but when God gets through with us, we have to do what he says. Many think the running will be over after we accept the calling, but some pastors still run every now and then. It is important to understand that we're not always running by choice. Sometimes the members, deacons, and trustees cause us to run.

Some may ask, "Run from what, Reverend?" Run from hard, piercing, and cutting messages that God sends to the church, but we're not always free to preach to them because of the repercussions we may have to suffer. So we run from that message for the people in fear of what may happen to us, just like Jonah. We don't always realize that when we run, God will deal with us, just like he dealt with Jonah when he ran.

So, Reverend, always preach the Word that God gives you, even if you have to preach it in tears on your way out the door!

You know, I've always found it strange how church folks can give preachers so much trouble, not realizing or caring that they have got it hard enough just doing what God wants them to do. You see, the problem is that people don't know everything the pastor preacher has gone through. They see the glamorous side of preaching, the monetary gifts, hugs, scattered love, recognition, and the elevation in ministry. Yes, they know about the glamour, but they don't know about the sleepless nights, the toiling and labor, the wet pillows at night, the loss of family time, the criticism and insults they have to endure, all the hindering spirits they have to fight, the days and nights traveling with no money in their pockets. Few people know what preachers have to go through. And in spite of all of this on Sunday morning, guess what? They have to push all of that aside and *preach* to a dying world.

Why? It's because preaching is above all. It's sad to say but preaching is more important than what they go through. Preaching is more important than how they feel. Preaching is so important that John lost his head. It's so important that Peter and the apostles kept doing it even though they were threatened and ended up in jail. It's so important that Paul decided, even in the face of death, to preach Jesus.

Preaching is so important that God told the prophet, "Your wife is going to die in the morning; bury her and in the evening PREACH to my people."

Preaching is so important that the Bible states that during one of Paul's long sermons, a man sitting in a high window fell asleep and dropped to the ground, but that didn't stop Paul. It had nothing to do with the preacher; preaching is so important because of the peril of the soul. Preachers continue to do what they do. And that's why preaching is a command. There is no choice. Pastors, you have to preach.

Tertullian said it best: "There is no other way to convert the world other than by the preaching of the gospel." There may be many ways to teach us how to succeed in life. There may be many ways that we are taught to preserve the economy and to enhance the temporal things in life. But there is only one way to turn man away from his sins, and that is what the apostle Paul calls the foolishness of preaching.

It has been said that the most effective way to diffuse religion is by preaching; not by the rituals of the church, and not by the human doctrines, because we can have a doctrine with no preaching. We can have laws with no preaching, but in order to convert folks from their sins, there must be preaching.

We cannot ignore the fact that Christianity owes its origin, its continuation, and its progress as it is to the act of preaching. It is preaching that has caused the cathedrals and synagogues to be built on millions of dollars. It is not the choir. It is not the church doctrine, it is the preaching of the gospel. It is preaching that caused the winos to lay down their liquor bottles. It is preaching that caused drug addicts to lay down their needles and crack pipes. It is preaching that pulls you up out of the muck and mire. It is biblical preaching that people need to hear on Sunday morning. People need to hear what God has done for them. They need to hear that God will open doors for them. They need to hear that God can heal their bodies. They need to hear that God can deliver them. They need to hear that God will touch them. They need to hear that God loves them. They need to hear that God cares for them, and most of all, they need to know that Jesus died just for them.

There is power in preaching. When Paul preached in Athens, they said, "His preaching turned the city upside down." Preaching gives life to any dead situation. When it looks like there is no hope, when it looks like there is nothing that can be done, preaching does strange things. Preachers must understand that there is power in the preached Word. Therefore, they must keep themselves protected by the Word of God. Preachers must keep themselves emerged in prayer, and every now and then, preachers need to be anointed so that the grace of God may rest upon them.

I want you to know that no preacher will be successful if they do not allow the Word of God to percolate their heart. If preachers don't study and seek higher learning through biblical training in this new age, they will have an unrelated message; their gospel will fall on deaf ears. They must remember that their calling is the highest calling in the world. It is the highest level in life: moral, social, and professional. To be one of God's chosen is indeed an honorable profession, even though some may object to the class and say, "He's just a preacher or he's just the pastor." God puts the highest regard on preachers because so much has been invested in them.

I want to remind you of the fact that doctors have been given a talent, but you can't find where God called the doctor. Lawyers practice the law, but you can't find where God called the lawyer. Magistrates judge the affairs of man, both right and wrong, but you can't find where God called the judge. But if you read the Bible, it tells you that God called Moses and said, "Moses, stop what you're doing, turn from where you're going, and come here. I've got a job for you. I've got work for you. I want you to go down to Egypt and tell Ol' Pharaoh to let my people go."

Preachers are emancipators. They are deliverers, and they have a message from God. They may not look like much to you, but their lips have been touched with tongues from the altar. Just like Aaron, they've had the oil poured on their head. Like Jeremiah, they've got the fire burning in their soul. Like Ezekiel, they have seen the vision of a dying people; they heard God say, "Ezekiel, can these bones live?" and Ezekiel said, "Lord, you know," and God said, "Ezekiel, *preach* until the graves come open, *preach* until the bones come out of the grave, *preach* until the head bone, the neck bone, the shoulder bone, the arm bone, the backbone, the hip bone, the thigh bone, the leg bone, the foot bone, the toe bone, all get together. Preach until the wind blows. Preach until Hell trembles. Preach until the storm rises."

Someone may be asking, "How shall I preach?" Preach in the name of the Lord. Preach in the strength of the Lord. Preach on the power of the Lord. The world is a valley of dry bones, but these dry bones can live if you preach. Every sinner can be saved and every drunk can be saved. If anybody ask you who told you to preach, if anybody asks you what you are doing, tell them, "I AM told me to preach! I AM told me to go! I AM told me to say it!" And no matter who comes or goes, PREACH!

Preachers have been called to do many things and to be many things to their people and their community. Preachers must understand that they are called to be a light and a leader, not only in the church but also in their community. The tragedy of the church today is that pastors have become selfish in the ministry and with the ministry. But the ministry that they are in is first of all not theirs. They are in the Lord's ministry, and it's a ministry of unity. Preachers should do the best that they can to bond with other ministries in the area, while at the same time maintaining their integrity.

It is together that we can tear down Satan's kingdom. They have been called to be at this place in the ministry known as pastor-ship, and above all they seek to do, they should never, ever forget that they have been given the command that God gave to Ezekiel. God commanded him to prophesy and preach.

CHAPTER 2

A Dual Responsibility
Who Is on Your Left and
Who Is on Your Right?

This chapter deals with the responsibility of the preacher to the people and the responsibility of the people to the preacher. It will be disturbing to those laypeople whose proclivity is not to honor the pastor, which is birthed out of ungodly teachings or their own analysis of the unworthiness of the preacher.

Many people do not understand when a day has been set aside to biblically honor the pastor. Many people do not understand why churches take time to honor their pastors. The real truth is some people do not even have a desire to honor the pastor of God's choosing. Churches suffer and many times perish because of the lack of the people's acceptance of knowledge. Sister Salle Mae Dew still engages in good old tongue speaking, crossover foot dancing, head shaking, body jerking, and long dress wearing; she is said to be saved, sanctified, Holy Ghost filled, and fire baptized, but she still raises the most hell. She refuses to give during any type of celebration (or honoring) for her pastor of fifteen years. We need to understand that it is God's will according to 1 Timothy 5:17 and also Hebrews 13:7:

> *Let the elders that rule well be counted worthy of double*
> *honor, especially they who labor in the word and doctrine.*
> 1 Timothy 5:17 (KJV)

7

> *Elders who do their work well should be paid well, especially those who work hard at both preaching and teaching.*
>
> 1 Timothy 5:17 (NLT)

> *Remember them which have the rule over you, who have spoken unto you the word of God: Whose faith follow, considering the end of their conversation.*
>
> Hebrews 13:7 (KJV)

> *Remember your leaders who first taught you the word of God. Think of all the good that has come from their lives, and trust the Lord as they do.*
>
> Hebrews 13:7 (NLT)

I am convinced that due to ignorance, the local church often misses the time God sets to honor and take care of the man of God. The tragedy of the church, the downfall of vision, and the stunted growth of ministry can be largely attributed to the church losing sight of the spiritual identity of its leaders.

As you sit and read this book, I only ask that you picture in your mind the face of your pastor and ask yourself, Who is this man? Not according to what you think, what you feel, or that which might be preprogrammed by disgruntled members along with what you heard about him, but according to what God says he is. Do you know in full revelation who your pastor is? For too long we have responded to pastors according to how we feel about them and what we think about them, and in response to the pastor's decision on matters or the aim of his messages.

At one time the children of Israel got upset about the way Moses was treating them, and they said that he was a hard task master; they thought it *seemed right* to respond to Moses according to the way he treated them.

We treat pastors accordingly because we feel it seems right. Yes, it may very well seem to us that we are right in the way we handle God's anointed; however, it would be wise to recall the words of

Proverbs 14:12: "There is a way which seemeth right unto a man. But the end thereof is the ways of death." Just because we feel something to be right in our spirit does not make it right. Proverbs 12:15 says, "The way of a fool is right in his own eyes, but he that harkeneth unto counsel is wise." Just because something is in your spirit does not mean that God put in there. 1 John 4:1 says, "Beloved, believe not every spirit, but try the spirits whether they are of God." We cannot respond to pastors like we handle *ordinary* men. In a spiritual sense, they are not ordinary.

This was something that Miriam had to find out the hard way. Miriam had the gall to rebuke and verbally scorn Moses because he married a Negro woman, a Cushite. In Numbers 12:1-5, you see that Aaron and Miriam were older than Moses, so Moses should have been subject to their authority. However, after the calling and work of God in the life of Moses, they ought to subject themselves to Moses' authority. They were not happy with the man of God's decision, so they thought it *seemed_right* to speak out against the leader, saying, "Hath Jehovah indeed spoken only with Moses? Hath He not also spoken with us?"

Now, what I'm trying to show you is that he was not an ordinary man. As his older sister, Miriam could have reprimanded her brother on the basis of their family relationship. But when she opened her mouth to slander him, she touched upon the work of God, challenging the position of Moses.

How wrong it was for Aaron and Miriam to attack Moses' position on the basis of a family reason. It was God who chose Moses (and it was God who chose your pastor). It was God who chose Moses to lead the people of Israel out of Egypt; nevertheless, Miriam despised him.

To the reader of this book, learn from Miriam that you cannot walk around despising the man of God. It's too upsetting to God and therefore too dangerous for you.

Because of Miriam's feelings toward Moses, God was very displeased with her. Strangely, she could deal with her brother, but she could never revile God's authority.

The trouble was that neither Aaron nor Miriam recognized God's authority. Therefore, they conceived a rebellious heart.

Yet Moses did not answer back. He knew that if he had been set up by God to be the authority, he need not defend himself. Whoever reviled him touched death. When we speak against our leader, our rebellious words ascend to heaven and are heard by God. Note this: when Aaron and Miriam sinned against Moses, they sinned against God, who was *in* Moses. (I'm still trying to figure out if you know who your pastor is.) The anger of the Lord was kindled against them (Numbers 12:9). Whenever man touches God's delegated authority, he touches God within that person. Sinning against delegated authority is sinning against God. And believe me, it has nothing to do with the man himself that God is so protective over; rather it's what's in the man. I will be the first to admit that it is a very hard thing to do, but for our life sake we must see beyond the physical man and recognize and yield to what is in the man.

Do you know who your pastor is? Can you see beyond the man to hear God? Just in case you cannot figure out the spiritual identity of your pastor, here are some titles to spiritually describe him.

Your pastor is:

- God's delegated authority
- God's anointed
- God's appointed
- God's mouthpiece
- God's representative
- God's vessel
- God's work
- God's instrument
- God's ambassador
- God's gift to the ministry
- God's own choosing
- God's ordained

He comes to you not just from the loins of his daddy, nor the womb of his mother, but just as it is written in Jeremiah 3:15, God has declared, "I will give you shepherds according to mine heart." He comes to you directly from the heart of God. His mother's womb was just the door he came through. Preachers must remember who they are and where they come from. Jesus always knew who he was, and when his family tried to hold him up, he said, "Wait a minute, woman, wish ye not that I be about my father's business" (in other words, "You're just the door I came through; I must be about my father's business").

So when I say that it is a dual responsibility, and that your responsibility is to your shepherd, I mean that you should look beyond the man to honor what God has put in the man. You're not making a God out of the man by honoring him or taking care of him. So never allow people stop you from doing what is in your spirit for the man of God.

A Dual Responsibility

The shepherd has a responsibility to the church (sheep), and the church has a responsibility to the shepherd. We are always conscious of the shepherd's responsibility to the sheep but unconscious of the church's responsibility to the shepherd.

The tragedy, particularly in the traditional church, is that we have missed the mark of caring for each other, because we have failed to understand that it is a command from God; it is not a choice that we must take care of each other. Pastors cannot look at the failures and shortcomings of the people and withdraw their commitment, their care, their display of love, their compassion, their understanding, their wisdom, their insight, and all of what God anointed them to pour into his people, which means that the pastor can never withdraw from the members. Pastors may tend to feel that it's not fair, because when the members get upset, they often withdraw. But the pastor can never withdraw. Members often have contrary ways, they are often ignorant, and they have shortcomings; every member of every congregation has some sin in them.

The preacher has been given a charge, and a charge the preacher must keep. We all understand the role of the pastor, but what the Body of Christ, particularly the traditional church, has failed to understand and carry out is that the sheep (the church) has a responsibility to the pastor, who is the shepherd, the angel over the house, regardless of the pastor's shortcomings. This means that in light of his failures, in light of his ignorance, in light of his stubbornness, in light of his imperfections, laity has a responsibility to the shepherd that they cannot back away from.

With all of your shortcomings, he cannot back away from his responsibility to you. No matter how hurt, angry, tired, frustrated, or fed up he may get, the shepherd still must fulfill his responsibility to the sheep. It is the same with the sheep: no matter how hurt, angry, tired, frustrated, or fed up you may get with the shepherd, you must fulfill your responsibility to your shepherd, because both the shepherd and the sheep will be held accountable to God.

We always focus on God holding the shepherd responsible, but for years the church has not realized that God holds them responsible for the man of God. Let me graciously throw this in: that's why church members must be very careful of how they recommend people to serve in governing positions in the church, because this puts people in the seat of accountability, particularly the office of the deacon and the office of trustee. Unless they are scripturally qualified as deacons, they should not be recommended or accepted. They must be saved, sanctified, and filled with the Holy Ghost. If they are not scripturally qualified, then the question is, have you really helped the pastor by giving him these people to labor with?

Hebrews tells us, "Blessed is he that makes the job of the pastor easier." Whenever you put non-spiritual people in a position to make spiritual decisions in the church, you have violated a spiritual law. The qualifications for deacons are found in scripture; however, the function of a trustee can be gleamed from different passages of the local church. Trustees help the pastor, who is the spiritual head and who tells us that the trustee should possess the same spiritual qualities as the deacon, which includes being saved, sanctified, and filled with the Holy Spirit in order to be a help to the spiritual head.

The reason I'm sharing this with you is that only these qualified people can lead you in fulfilling your responsibility of taking care of your shepherd.

Now for your consideration, look at Galatians 6:6-7, because it points out the responsibility of all people who sit under the teaching of any pastor. Romans 15:27 and 1 Corinthians 9:11 basically tell us the same thing: "Let him that is taught in the word communicate or share with him that teacheth in all good things." This text tells us that as our teacher pours out of himself the teachings of the gospel, we must pour back into his life.

The church has the responsibility of taking good care of the pastor. The fact is that we have not faithfully done this, and as a result we have seen the withering of anointed leaders in the church. The bottom line is that it is wrong for your pastors to minister to you and for you to receive what they teach without reciprocating back into their life. It is wrong for them to bless, change, and alter you without you communicating back to them. It is wrong for them to pastor you and teach you and pour their life into you for years without you pouring your life back into them.

Let him that receiveth teaching note that is the first responsibility in this text. The pastor is responsible for teaching you. After you have been taught, you should communicate back unto him in all good things. You must understand that when you fail to pour back into him, it will create weariness in him, because he will always be pouring out, and no one will be putting anything back into the man of God.

There must be a system of reciprocating going on. We are here today to raise money, but other commentaries declare that this reciprocating is not only talking about money. There must be compassion, care, expressed love, concern, loyalty, and strengthening. (And money poured from you back to your pastor.)

It is a dual responsibility, and when we fail to do it, we again violate a spiritual law.

We cannot continue ignoring this command, because Galatians 6:7 says, "Be not deceived; God is not mocked; whatsoever a man soweth that shall he also reap." Now usually when we quote this passage of scripture, we are heralding it at someone who we feel has done us wrong, but when you put it in context, it is indeed the very next verse after the command for us to give unto our man of God. The commentary says this verse refers to the foregoing exhortation to convince those of their sin and folly that endeavored to excuse themselves from doing their duty in supporting their ministers. It is a sin to ignore your leader and not give unto him.

It is undoubtedly known that the sheep need a shepherd but often forgotten that the shepherd needs the sheep as well.

CHAPTER 3

The Pain and Joy of the Assignment & The Value of Your Ministry Jeremiah 1:1-10; 20:1-9

Here is the story of a diffident, sensitive young man who was called from the obscurity of his native town to assume, at a critical hour in the nation's life, the overwhelming responsibilities of a prophet.

Jeremiah came from the village of Anathoth, some three miles from Jerusalem. This gave him the advantage of the Holy City. His father, Hilkiah, was a priest. He inherited the traditions of an illustrious ancestry. His early life was, no doubt, molded by strong religious influences. But God had something better for Jeremiah than to spend his life as a priest serving at the altars. God appointed this young man to be a prophet of the Lord in this most trying hour in the history of the chosen people.

God often chooses unlikely instruments to do his work. He chose the sensitive, shrinking Jeremiah for what seemed a hopeless mission, with the words: "Do not say I am only a child. You must go to everyone I send you to and say whatever I command you. Do not be afraid of them, for I am with you and I will rescue you, declares the Lord" (Jeremiah 1:7-8). This is what a prophet is: one who says what God tells him to. Although many prophets foretold future events, this is not necessary.

Jeremiah, unlike many of the prophets, had much to say concerning himself. He was a priest by birth (1:1). He was called by the Lord to be a prophet at an early age (1:6). He pleaded, first, his youth (only twenty-one); second, his inexperience; and third, his lack of eloquence (1:6) as reasons for not accepting the call. Are these not just the excuses that youth make today for not obeying Christ?

Jeremiah was assured that Jehovah ordained him to this work before his birth (1:5). God tells us in Ephesians 2:10 that we were created unto good works before God even laid the foundation of the world. God has a plan for each one of our lives (Jeremiah 1:1-8). He was not allowed to marry, for God had a special mission for him in life (16:1-2). Jeremiah prophesied during the time when Israel had been taken into captivity and Judah was in her declining days.

Jeremiah's message was never a popular one. At one time he barely escaped with his life (26:7-16). There was another time where his enemies beat him and put him in prison. Men have always treated God's witnesses this way.

When you study the book of Jeremiah, you will find that there was a great contest for world supremacy in his day. Assyria had been in the place of leadership for three hundred years. Now she was growing weak, Babylon was ascending in power, and Egypt was striving for supremacy. Assyria was defeated by Babylon. Egypt was crushed in the battle of Carchemish, and Babylon became the world's master. In the years that followed, she invaded Jerusalem and took the Jews captive. False prophets swarmed the city of Jerusalem in these days. They flattered the king and prophesied to him whatever they thought he wanted to hear.

So now there was a need for what God had preordained to come into fruition. The hidden call and assignment inside a normal young man must be awakened, for the fullness of time that he should come forth was at hand. This unique tragedy, as one writer calls it, was a call to pain and glory that opened in the little village of Anathoth.

Jeremiah became aware that God had ordained him before his birth, without his consent, to be a prophet. God already has a plan for your life. Some see clearly how their lives are to be used. Some learn to wait upon God and trust him for the outcome.

Upon receiving instructions, Jeremiah spoke out against the call and assignment. He acknowledged that God is sovereign but he still said, "I can't speak, I'm only a child." This reminds me of Moses in Exodus 4:10-12: "And Moses said unto the Lord, 'O, my Lord, I am not eloquent, either in the past or since you have spoken unto thy servant(ESV): but I am slow of speech, and of tongue.' And the Lord said unto him, 'Who hath made man's mouth, or who maketh the dumb, or deaf, or the seeing or the blind? Have not I the Lord?' Then the Lord said, 'Now therefore go and I will be with your mouth, and teach you what you should say.'" Like Jeremiah looking at his assignment, Moses said to God, "Lord, please send someone else!"

God called, and Jeremiah protested and shrank from the assignment and begged God to be excused. You can't help but notice Jeremiah's reluctance to undertake the assignment.

Why the reluctance? It's not like he had to create great speeches out of his own wit. A prophet is simply God's messenger, delivering not his own ideas but conveying to the last detail God's thoughts. Well, that's where you get in trouble, with humanity saying what God tells you! John lost his head, Paul and Silas were put in prison, Moses was on the run with an army on his trail, John was exiled to Patmos, and Jeremiah's own father and brother wanted to kill him.

But this was the task that God called Jeremiah to, and finally he entered into it bravely. But he was overwhelmed at the thought of hurting anyone. He would rather just live at peace with everyone. Jeremiah said, "I have not reached the years of maturity."

You see, in the Middle East, a young man had no role to play until he was of age. His prophetic message would not be received. He knew that his career would be cut short by those he provoked. He knew that they would try to kill him.

Jeremiah was conscious of his inexperience and almost refused. But God knows how to overcome our hesitancy. He made the young Jeremiah conscious of a divine call. He made Jeremiah able to see that the work to which he was assigned was not his own. (I wonder how many of us understand that our ministry is not our own!)

One writer declared that the path of duty is the path of safety; the songwriter declared that the safest place is in the will of God.

While Jeremiah was pondering, a hand touched his mouth, and a voice said, "Now, I have put my words in your mouth." Jeremiah lost his excuse of being unable to speak. God promises to put a word in the mouth of his prophets. And then Jeremiah heard the voice give him assignment: "Today I give you the assignment to stand up against nations and kingdoms. You are assigned to uproot some and tear them down, to destroy and overthrow them. You are assigned to build others up and plant them."

God began to load Jeremiah down with his concerns; he began to present his case against his people.

He gave Jeremiah the results of Israel's sin. Then, he presented Israel as an unfaithful wife. Next, he told Jeremiah that Judah was following Israel's example and that treacherous Judah was worse than faithless Israel. So he told Jeremiah of the coming judgment against Judah. Jeremiah tried to deal with the pain and wept for his people (his nickname was "weeping prophet"). God gave him a sneak preview and a vision of the coming disaster. God mentioned Judah's sins and assigned Jeremiah to make an announcement to Israel and Judah, calling them senseless and foolish. Jeremiah dealt with the pain of seeing Israel dwell in constant rebellion and reject the Lord's way. Jeremiah dealt with attacks and invasion from the north, and then he told them about being wicked and hiding in the temple.

Jeremiah wrestled with the shame of looking like a liar. All of this prophesy, and yet the one whom he spoke on behalf of, the one who gave him every word that he had spoken, had not yet done what he told Jeremiah. To prophesy, oh, how much pain we would escape if God would get in a hurry and do quickly what he spoke into our spirit. Oftentimes preachers say, "God, do it quickly, it would make it easier for your prophets." It's painful when the process is not in your favor.

We often approach an assignment with a spirit that is as weary as our physical condition. An unspoken thought often takes up residence in our mind; that thought is nestled in the subdued or suppressed department of our mind. We do not speak this thought aloud, but it's hanging somewhere over our head.

We can't share it with other preachers, because half of them don't like us and are awaiting our demise. We dare not tell our members, because some of them have members in our church who are on our roll but are not our members yet. This group jointly holds the dagger that has us bleeding; we can't share this thought with them, for they are devoid of empathy toward us and our vision.

The silent question is there in our mind. We know what we heard in the spirit realm, and we know the sovereign voice of God. We have learned how to distinguish the vast difference between the finite thoughts in our head and the authentic voice of God. And after hearing God, the problem is what he says to us through the spirit realm has not yet come to fruition in the natural realm, like Jeremiah.

It's painful and frustrating when what we are looking at has no resemblance to what he has said. It's frustrating when he allows us to see our sanctuary full beyond capacity, but the reality is only 40 percent of the seats are occupied. It's frustrating when he convinces us that it's going to get better and allows us to envision it but does not allow us to see it.

You hear one thing, but for years you're beholding another. You see one thing but in reality you're standing on the binary opposite! Frustration! You have a sovereign God who spoke and said it is. But time and reality say not yet. And the question jumping in your mind after all these years is, Is God toying with me?

The needs of your people and community are calling for fruition of all that you have seen and heard, leaving you wondering what in the world is going on.

You are nowhere near what you saw, so you have to fight to be where you are! And the worst thing is, you don't have the liberty to turn in a resignation to God. He is just like he is and will not remove the assignment.

So the first part of the pain of the assignment is that you are stuck in the assignment. Next, you are sent to folks who will kill you because of the message. Then, you end up friendless. Also, you suffer but not alone. Your family never gives a prophet what he deserves. There is also the pain of trying to take people someplace they don't want to go. Lastly, God won't let you quit.

However:

- The joy is like Jeremiah. He will deliver you from your oppressors.
- The call is divine. It's God, the sovereign one, God, Jehovah, God that answers by fire, God the Almighty that has hand-picked you out of his heart.
- The joy is knowing that God is with you and has promised to be your rescuer.
- The joy is knowing that although you can't quit, one day, like Paul, you will finish and get a crown and forever be with the Lord.

So we endure the pain, realizing that through it all, the prophets are held in God's protective hands.

CHAPTER 4

Who Cares if You Die?
Acts 9:36-41

Life is filled with many things. It is filled with days of joy, days of sadness, and worries. It is filled with dreams, with aspirations, and most of all with something that is oftentimes unmet, and that is purpose. Many people live without tapping into their God-given purpose. God has created each one of us with a purpose: "Our chief purpose is to live for God, to do good, and help those that are in need." Jesus said in Matthew 25:34-40, "In as much as ye have done it unto the least of these my brethren, ye have done it unto me." Then he said, "Ye are my disciples when you show love one to another." What Jesus was saying is that when you have done these things, you have filled your purpose.

When we fulfill our purpose, it will not only affect us as individuals, it will also affect those who come in contact with us. A life that is consecrated to God is supposed to be a life consecrated to service, serving your fellow man.

When I asked the question who cares if you die, first of all, I knew that nobody wants to talk about death, particularly their own death.

Perhaps that's the problem in the Body of Christ; we often forget that we must one day die. We will not live this life forever. Every one of us has a date with the dust. The reservation has already been made, without the privilege of cancellation.

Hebrews 9:27 said that "as it is appointed unto men once to die but after this the judgment"; so you've got to die. That's not the question; the question is, who cares?

Peter, with his anointed self, softly called the name of Dorcas, raising her from the dead. I don't want to focus on Dorcas, but I am concerned about the people in the room after her death. In the ninth chapter of Acts, we have a delightful story beginning with verse 36: "Now they were at Joppa (Joppa is not far from Lydda, and is on the sea coast, whereas Lydda is inland) a certain disciple named Tabitha, which by interpretation is called Dorcas. It is said that Dorcas may have been one of the early converts of Phillip the evangelist, who established a Christian church in Joppa. This woman was full of good works and full of alms, a deed which she did."

I want to fix your attention on that for a few moments. This is very real evidence of a truly converted person.

Consecrated, she was deeply interested in doing good to others. I am afraid sometimes we forget that side of it. Many believers are so terribly self-centered. Some seem to be looking constantly for some new religious thrill or new spiritual experience. Some are always looking inside and always seeking blessings for themselves, and they throng the inquiry room when the invitation is given for Christians who want a little more than they have. If you gave the invitation a hundred times, no matter how much we have at the invitation to get more, we keep coming. The question is why do we want more.

This isn't the ideal Christian at all. The ideal Christian is one who is resting in Christ for his soul's salvation. Now your great concern is not your own salvation, but that of others. John insists on this, and James asks, "If a brother or sister be naked, and destitute of daily food, and one of you say unto them, Depart in peace, be ye warmed and filled; notwithstanding ye give them not those things which are needful to the body, what doth it profit?"

This woman, Tabitha, loved the Lord and manifested it in a very practical way. She was not satisfied with reading the Word only, but she had a consecrated needle and used it for the blessing of other people; the Spirit of God has preserved this record that we might learn from it and never forget it. Some of us Christians are satisfied and should be, but those who are not satisfied with their life, get busy and try to help and bless other people, and you will be surprised to see how your own spiritual condition will improve! You will get along wonderfully well when you start thinking about others.

Anyone constantly occupied with his own spiritual experience and never concerned about blessing other people will never have an experience worth being occupied with.

This woman Dorcas must have been a most genuine person. Now, I can't imagine her as one of these arrogant saints we sometimes see today; going around with long, melancholy faces and a "holier-than-thou" attitude. I think her face gleamed with the love of Christ. I do not think she had a dainty little handshake, nor did she have a bad air about herself, but I believe she had a pump-handle handshake. She was always interested in other people: truly a warm-hearted Christian.

Study says that Tabitha must have been a woman of wealth or had connections with wealth. But this woman died, her spirit went home to be with Christ, and her body lay there in an upper room. "And it came to pass in those days, that she was sick, and died." The Christians on one hand felt that Dorcas should go to heaven, but they wanted her here.

Paul said, "It's better for me to get out of here and it's better for you if I stay." What Paul was saying is that my life has been a benefit to you. For some of us, they would not worry very much. They would just look pious and say, "The Lord gave and the Lord has taken him away." But they would not be very anxious to have us come back. These believers, however, were exceedingly sorry to lose this wonderful Christian character (Dorcas).

"And forasmuch as Lydda was nigh to Joppa, and the disciples had heard that Peter was there, they sent unto him two men, desiring him that he would not delay to come to them." They probably thought, "We do not know what he can do, but we shall send for him." "Then Peter arose and went with him. When he was come, they brought him into the upper chamber: and all the widows stood by him weeping, and showing the coats and garments which Dorcas made while she was with them." Can't you just see that picture? There is the body of the dear one who is gone, lying upon a couch, dead, and here are her friends mourning for her.

One tells Peter, "Look at this garment of mine. I don't know where I was going to get a winter coat, but she cut a coat that her grandfather left and made it over for me!" And others were showing one thing after another: "Dorcas made it for me!" These people astonish me as they testify about the value of Dorcas's life. Sometimes your value is measured not by what you have inside, but rather what you pour out. These garments seemed to have a voice, but Peter heard their crying and "put them all forth, and kneeled down, and prayed: and turned him to the body and said, Tabitha, arise."

And she opened her eyes, and when she saw Peter, she sat up. And he gave her his hand (perfect gentlemen that he was) and lifted her up, and when he had called the saints and widows, he presented her alive. Ah, what a rejoicing they must have had!

Three Points

1. Live out your purpose.
2. Live so that there is somebody who doesn't want you to die.
3. Live so that God will work miracles in your life.

God caused her to live again to continue doing something; consider these questions:

> *Why should God heal you?*
> *Why should God raise you?*
> *Why should God turn your dead situation around?*
> *Why should God anoint you?*
> *Why should God give you wisdom?*

Note this: What looks like death God will reverse.

David: after committing adultery
Ezekiel: in the valley of dead bones
Peter: after denying Christ
Paul: after the shipwreck
Jonah: in the fish's belly in the bottom of sea.
You and I: after (you name it . . .)

I want somebody to miss me when I'm gone. I want God to have to raise up somebody with a heart of compassion for people who no longer have because of my departure. The value of Dorcas's life to the people is why they cared. I wonder if there is anybody who cares if you die. Is there anybody who says you were there when I needed a friend? You were there in my days of sickness? You were there when I had no money? You were there when my son died? You were there when my wife died? You were there when my husband died? You were there when I thought I would lose my mind? You were there when I was tired and needed someone to drive for me? You were there when others left me? You helped me when no one else would, and I care if you die?

You taught me how to:

love
live
forgive
go
never give up
trust God!

CHAPTER 5

Evangelism
Where Are the Fishers?

I have never been interested in fishing; it could never hold my attention. Being out in a boat or sitting on a dock holding a rod with a string hanging from it all day in the sun is no fun for me. Running from water moccasins, fighting mosquitoes, and being surrounded by the threat of everything else that is not human, I'm having trouble seeing the fun in all of this. Therefore, I fish at the local fish market.

However, contrary to my cloudy view of fishing as a sport, there are those who live to have their time at the dock or on the boat fishing. For many people, young and old, fishing is an outlet. It is sincere relaxation. It clears their mind. It takes away their frustration. It holds a high place on their to-do list.

There are people whose only source of income is what they pull in on their boats. The sport of fishing has retired a lot of people from their secular jobs. Fishing tournaments have put thousands of dollars in professional fishermen's pockets. Believe it or not, there are many people who have actually chosen fishing as their lifelong occupation.

Fishing is not new. It is an ancient trade. It is a trade found in the following text.

This second call of the apostle Peter is apparently the same incident that is recorded in the first chapter of the gospel according to Mark. Simon had met Jesus prior to this incident in this chapter, and he had come to call him his Savior, but then he had gone about his business again as if nothing had happened. (When you receive Christ, the rest of your life is not business as usual, it's new business.) Peter had continued his fishing career, as usual, and there seems to have been no outward change in his life.

On this particular morning, Peter and the boys, were tired and disgusted; they had returned from an all night fishing trip without a single fish. They were not on the boat when Jesus stepped on the scene; they were washing their nets when Jesus interrupted them and commandeered Simon's ship. Jesus seized Simon's ship to act as sort of a pulpit from which to teach the great multitudes who had come to hear him. Now after the sermon, Jesus then ordered Simon to pull away from the shore and to let down the nets.

Once you come to this dock to be taught, you must then pull away from the dock and do what you have been taught. Jesus told Simon to pull away from the dock and drop his nets. But Simon strongly objected and reminded the Lord that it was of no use, because they had fished all night long and had not caught one single fish. But the Lord had something quite different in mind than nets full of ordinary fish. In this text, Simon is getting ready to learn a new lesson; he was now ready for the great lesson of discipleship.

Now I want you to notice and understand the play on the names in this text, because it is significant. This great lesson is immediately suggested by the repeated use of the name "Simon," without the surname "Peter" in this passage. Now, remember that this was not Peter's first encounter with Jesus; at a previous time Jesus had already met and changed Peter's name from Simon to Peter, so in close study of this passage, notice and underscore each time the name "Simon" occurs.

First we are told in verse 3 that Jesus entered "Simon's" boat (not Simon Peter). Then in the next verse Jesus says to "Simon" (not Peter): "Launch out into the deep." Again in verse 5 we read, "And Simon [again not Peter] answering said unto him, Master, we have toiled all the night, and have taken nothing." It is not until verse 8 where he falls down at Jesus' feet that his full name, "Simon Peter," is used. This is significant indeed. I believe every word in this record was carefully chosen by the Holy Spirit. Dr. Luke is giving it to us just as he received it. There must be some design, some specific purpose in the careful use of the name, Simon, over and over again, without the usual surname, Peter.

The reason becomes evident when we remember that "Simon" was the name his natural father, John, had given Peter. Simon represents the old man of the flesh, by his first birth. Simon had come to Christ and become Peter, but in our scripture we see little evidence of the "Peter," for it is all Simon, all flesh. It is "Simon" from beginning to end. It was Simon who had toiled all night in his own strength. It was into Simon's boat that Jesus chose to enter, to set the stage for the much-needed lesson Simon was about to learn. It was to Simon that Jesus said, "Launch out into the deep, and let down your nets for a draught."

Here is Simon's fleshly answer, and remember it is Simon speaking, and not Peter. He asks in essence, "Excuse me, Mr. Jesus, but you want us to let down the nets after we have just finished washing them? First, Mr. Jesus, the fish aren't biting; it's no use, Lord, I am an old experienced fisherman, and you have never been a fisherman, and I assure you it will do no good. These boys and I have toiled all night and caught nothing. It's no use. If we couldn't catch them during the night, it certainly is a waste of energy to try it in broad daylight. Secondly, we have just finished washing our nets and now you want us to soil our nets again, and for no good purpose?"

Now, all of this was from Simon, the man of the flesh, the old man who disputed the very words of the One who made the sea and the fish. The flesh is not of faith, and Simon had no faith in his Master's advice. He walked by sight and reason, and not by faith. What a lesson Simon had to learn! Now, while he insisted it was no use to let down the nets, he protestingly added, and this is very interesting:

"Nevertheless at thy word I will let down the net" (Luke 5:5).

This was not an act of obedience, as may appear on the surface, but an act of absolute unbelief. Simon seems to say, "I know it will do no good, but just to prove, Lord, how mistaken you are, I will let down just one net." But Jesus had said to Simon that his vision was big); Jesus always sees the greater harvest.

Let Down the Nets

Not only one of them, but all of them, because you will need every one of them. The word is plural, "nets." But Simon says, "That's foolish, Lord. One net is going to be enough to prove how wrong you are. There certainly is no use letting down more than one. There simply are no fish over there, but I will let down the net, one net, to prove it."

This was the reasoning of Simon after the flesh. If you're going to be fishers of men, you have to get out of the flesh. You see, you will never hear what God says can be done if the only senses you have are fleshly senses.

But as we read the text, we see that after Simon dropped the net, and then came the surprise. Now the multitude of fish was so great that the net broke. The net was ruined because Simon had caught in one net the fish that should have been caught in many nets. Oh, just think about what he could have had if he had done it according to the Master's plan.

In this connection, we call attention to another incident when Peter let down another net at the command of the Lord and enclosed a tremendous amount of fishes. Yet in this instance, the net did not break. You will find the record in John 21. It is after the resurrection, and again Peter and the disciples had spent a fruitless night fishing after Peter had given up all hope that Jesus Christ was coming back again. He had gone back again to the energy of the flesh, and then once more Jesus appears on shore, and says to Peter:

"Cast the net on the right side of the ship" (John 21:6). When they had cast the net as Jesus ordered, they filled a net with great fishes (153 large fish) and "For all there were so many, yet was not the net broken" (John 21:11).

In this case, the net did not break. Why not a broken net in this case, as in Luke? The answer is simply because the first instance was done in disobedience. For Jesus had said, "Let down the nets," and Simon had let down only one. But in this last instance, Jesus had commanded them to let down only one net, and it held. Everything done in the flesh must fail. Only that which is done in complete obedience and faith in the Lord Jesus can succeed. And so Peter had to learn the first great lesson of discipleship: absolute, complete obedience to the will of the Master. Failure to do so can only result in loss.

Now Comes Peter

Now to return to our narrative in Luke 5. Simon saw the tremendous catch of fishes and the broken net, and the boat sinking under the weight of the catch; he suddenly seemed to come to his senses. He realized what a terrible mistake he had made. He felt the awfulness of his willful, fleshly action, and so we read:

When Simon Peter saw it, he fell down at Jesus' knees, saying, "Depart from me; for I am a sinful man, O Lord" (Luke 5:8).

In other words, the man who had argued with the Lord, disputed his Word, the man who had sarcastically said, "Because you won't believe me, I'll have to prove it to you, and let down just one net," now fell in repentance at Jesus' feet, confessed his awful sinfulness, repented, and called him Lord. It is interesting in this connection to note that in verse 5, Simon called Jesus "Master" and said, "Master, we have toiled all the night, and have taken nothing."

When Peter comes to the place of complete and full obedience and repentance, however, he drops the name, Master, and he calls him Lord. That is the first prerequisite of discipleship: to recognize the absolute Lordship of Jesus Christ. Then, too, do not miss the point that up until the eighth verse, the name "Simon" is used each time he is referred to, but when Simon comes to the place of acknowledging him as Lord, the name Peter occurs. This is the new nature that is now coming to the forefront, the new man of the spirit who is willing to follow the Lord Jesus Christ.

This is a passage that carries a tremendous lesson for all of us. The man who had argued with the Lord is now ready to follow him all the way.

The Crisis in Peter's Life

This was a crisis in Simon's life. Notice carefully that it was Simon who went fishing, it was Simon who caught nothing, it was Simon who disputed with the Lord, but when we read of Simon's repentance, confession, and acknowledgment of him as lord, it is Peter who is speaking. Now the new nature reveals itself. Before it had been all flesh, all Simon, Simon, Simon. But now coming to the surface, and to the forefront, is the new nature, Peter.

Only after the new Peter had gained the victory over the old Simon did Jesus reveal the great lesson he had in mind when he performed this miracle. He was not interested merely in the fish, but in something far more important.

And Jesus said unto Simon, "Fear not; from henceforth thou shalt catch men" (Luke 5:10).

Here then is a brand new commission, a new experience, an additional blessing. Simon Peter, the believer, now becomes Peter the disciple. He had come to Jesus for salvation. Now he is to follow after him for service, and we read:

"And when they had brought their ships to land, they forsook all, and followed Him" (Luke 5:11).

They Forsook All

Now, salvation is free and costs us nothing. For it cost him his all. But discipleship is quite a different matter. It means full surrender, complete yielding, and a forsaking of self to follow him.

31

It means absolute, unquestioning obedience to his will. This is the greatest need in the church today. There are all too few "disciples" who are willing to pay the price of service and victory.

There are thousands of believers who, like Simon before this crisis in his life came, just go on day after day, week after week, without power or fruit, while the few devoted, surrendered disciples do all the work and sacrificing, and of course, get most of the blame when things go wrong. The average Christian is just a "hitchhiker' on the way to heaven. A few others have to do the driving, the pushing and the pulling, and the toiling; they have to pay for the gas, and endure the rejection, and try to keep themselves encouraged, while the rest just ride along, singing about salvation, testifying about their glorious Lord, but knowing nothing about discipleship. But the first thing we must figure out stems from verse 2, which says when Jesus got to the boat the fishermen were gone out of them!

It is a matter of history that all the mighty servants of the Lord, who were greatly used of God, came in the course of their Christian experience to just such a crisis as Simon did. Subsequent to their conversion, they came to the place where the flesh had to be repudiated, to the place where in full and complete surrender, they gave their all to him. And so we ask, is Jesus your Savior only, or have you also owned him fully as Lord and Master of your entire life? He wants to be the Lord of your life, because he knows that only in that way can you get the very best he has for you. It is only such whom he will use. It is a matter of record that it is the disciples, those who have owned the Lordship of Christ, who have been used as gold in the promotion of the work he has committed to his followers.

May God help us to face the question honestly, because there is a judgment seat of Christ coming. When shall we have to give an account to him? Am I living a life that is less than God's best for me? Am I missing something the Lord wants me to have? Do I go week after week or month after month, without seeing progress?

Is my life without power, fruit, joy, and assurance? Then I need the experience of Simon Peter.

Search your own heart, and ask yourself whether there is any progress in your Christian life since you were saved. The fishers were not in the boat, they were washing their nets.

CHAPTER 6

The Necessity of the Preacher
Romans 10:14

There are many things in this world provided for us that can be considered necessities, and then there are some things that can only be considered luxuries. Oftentimes we fail at distinguishing the difference between necessities and luxuries. Many times our luxuries become our necessities. In a broader sense, we understand that due to the fact that as we live, our bodies go through health changes; therefore, we readily agree that medical doctors are a necessity to society. We can also agree that due to the fact that man is not always trustworthy, and handshakes no longer seal business transactions, that lawyers are a necessity in society. What else can we agree on? We can agree that man is not always just in settling the affairs for other men; therefore, it necessitates the need of judges and the judicial system. The list could go on and on, but I think you get the picture.

Romans 10:14 shares with us the necessity of the preacher. It says, "How, then, can they call on the one they have not believed in? And how can they believe in the one of whom they have not heard? And how can they hear without someone preaching to them?" In this one verse Paul nutshells the necessity of all preachers of the gospel.

Understanding the sinful nature of humanity, the spiritual deadness, and the spiritual deafness of all persons who have not been born again, we see the need of an awakening. In the natural world, we awaken each other by a physical shaking, the sound of an alarm clock, or raising the shades, allowing the bright sun to shine in our faces. But in order to have an awakening out of the dead and state of sin, there must be a spiritual awakening, a conversion (saving of the soul) that is only done through the Word of God. God has decided that men are only saved by the foolishness of preaching (1 Corinthians 1:21), which takes us back to the necessity of the preacher.

When we look carefully at Romans 10:14, it is a response of Paul to questioning Jews. Paul had already explained to them that the way to God was not through works or living by the law. He told them that the only way was through faith and trust. After hearing Paul, they asked, "What if the Jews never heard of that?" So actually in Romans 10:14, Paul is addressing the question.

1). You cannot call on God unless you *believe* in him.
2). You cannot believe in him unless you *hear* about him.
3). You cannot *hear* about him unless there is someone to *preach* the good news.
4). There can be no one to preach the good news unless God *calls* them to do so.

Notice how everything hinges on the necessity of the preacher.

To further examine the necessity of the preacher, let's glance quickly at Isaiah 61:1-3:

> *"The spirit of the Lord God is upon me, because the Lord hath anointed me to preach good tidings unto the meek; He hath sent me to bind up the broken hearted, to proclaim liberty to the captives, and the opening of the prison to those who are bound; To proclaim the acceptable year of the Lord, and the day of vengeance of our God; to comfort all that mourn; To appoint unto those who mourn in Zion, to give unto them beauty for ashes, the oil of joy for mourning, the garment of praise for the spirit of heaviness, that they might be called trees of righteousness, the planting of the Lord, that He might be glorified."*

35

This can be a troubling passage of scripture because you have to figure out who is doing the speaking. Although Isaiah was the messenger who proclaimed liberty to the Jews in Babylon, so was the Lord Jesus Christ. We draw our conclusion that in this particular text, the person being spoken of by the Eagle Eye Prophet is Jesus Christ; consider Luke 4:17-21:

> *"And there was delivered unto him [Jesus] the book of the prophet Isaiah. And when He had opened the book, He found the place where it was written, The spirit of the Lord is upon me, because he hath anointed me to preach the gospel to the poor; he hath sent me to heal the brokenhearted, to preach deliverance to the captives, and recovering of sight to the blind, to set at liberty them that are bruised, To preach the acceptable year of the Lord. And He closed the book, and He gave it again to the minister, and sat down. And the eyes of all them that were in the synagogue were fastened on Him. And He began to say unto them. This day is this scripture fulfilled in your ears."*

My Pastor
Dr. Howard Eugene McNair Sr.

Pastor of the New Stoney Hill United Holy Church Goldsboro,
N.C. for over 50 years.

CHAPTER 7

Going the Full Measure
(Tribute to Dr. H. E. McNair Sr.)
Luke 9:23-26 Luke 12:22-23

In this life, there are always those who will never go any further than you carry them. They will never go any further than they are carried, told to go, or driven. Somehow they do not have what it takes to go all the way. Whether it is in Christian life or in temporal life, they just never go the full measure. In this Christian life, we must decide whether we are preparing ourselves to be a continuous Christian or just one of these part-timers who are just here for as long as it seems good, looks good, and feels good. You probably know some folk like that. It's got to seem good; things have to be well with them all the time. There are those who are looking for the flowery beds of leaves, complimentary words, and pats on the backs. Then there are those who are always looking for the feeling. No reality whatsoever. They just want to feel something. In all reality, all of us who name the name of Jesus Christ must come to understand that Christ requires us to prepare ourselves to go the full measure. This message shows throughout the pages of God's Word. God himself went the full measure in creating this world. He put everything in it that the human eye wants or that is possible for a human to desire; he didn't leave anything out. When he made the world, he put everything in it. Any type of fruit, any type of herb, anything we would need in this life, God put it in this world. I don't know why NASA keeps sending folks to the moon. When you think about it, when he grew a tree, he grew a house, a church, a chair. Lord have mercy! When he made vegetation, he made it possible for us to be sustained with nourishment; he also filled the ocean with water. It wasn't just for the fish, and it wasn't just to beautify the world—he did it for us. No wonder David said, "The earth is the Lord's and the fullness thereof and they that dwell therein." And when he had completed his works, he saw that it was good and very good. In creating man, he went a little further than that. He did not make man like anything else that existed. He wanted to do something different. "Let us make man in our own image and likeness." He went the full measure.

Now I know what the evolutionists say. They say we came from apes, monkeys, and baboons, but I've got news for you. I came from God. God made me out of the dust of the earth, fashioned me with his own hand, blew his breath into me, and I became a living soul. And this is the fact you must seek to teach in your church, in your home, in your school, and everywhere you are; if they can teach evolution, we can teach Creation. Tell your children where they came from. Tell them God made them. Tell them that's God's breath that they're breathing. Tell them that's God strength that they're using. So many young people take life for granted because they don't know its source. He went the full measure. Made me like him. You ought to tell God thank you. You want to know what God looks like? He looks like us. He made us like him. He not only gave us an image like him, he also made us inwardly like him.

He went the full measure. Adam, who was very much like God in the flesh and the total likeness of God himself, failed the creator. He damaged his image. He caused the God who had formed man out of the dust of the earth to disown him and vanish him out of his sight forever. And a curse was placed upon him. God not only cursed man, but he also cursed woman. God not only cursed the woman, he also cursed the serpent. And he told man, "From this day forward, you are going to earn your living by the sweat of your brow." We've been working ever since. He told the woman she was going to labor in child bearing; a woman is closer to death when she brings a child into the world than she is at any other time in her life. He looked at that serpent, which the devil had slipped his spirit into, and cursed him and said, "From this day forth shall you crawl on your belly and eat the dust of the earth."

Now, that sounds to me like he was walking upright, walking like I walk, standing up like I'm standing. But when the devil beguiled him and he deceived Eve, she gave the apple to Adam, and he disobeyed God, God cursed all of them!

The fact is that man was the delight of his eye. He failed them. His own image and likeness lay down in the pit touched by the hand of Satan. But our loving Lord went the full measure. John 3:16 says, "God so loved the world that he gave his only begotten Son, that whosoever believeth in Him shall not perish but have everlasting life." He went the full measure. In the Old Testament there are Bible characters who in their own way were called upon to go the full measure and did so for God, without any questions. But there are those who had to go through all kinds of difficulties, but by the help of the almighty God, they did it in their day and in their time. And so must we do in this day and in this time. Listen to what the hymn writer says: "Must Jesus bear the cross alone and all the world go free? No, there is a cross for everyone, there's a cross for me."

Allow me to lift a few Old Testament characters:

First, we have Moses, who went the full measure. He chose to suffer the afflictions with the people of God, rather than be called the son of Pharaoh's daughter. He indeed went the full measure. Jonah was brought to the wilderness. As he went down, he became willing to go the full measure. Sometimes many of us can't go up until we do down. You know, sometimes the Lord has to bring us down before he brings us up. He has to carry us down before he brings us out. And some of us have to go down so that we can know that only God can bring us out.

The Bible tells me that God spoke to Jonah and told him to go to Nineveh and preach the gospel; because of the fate of the other prophets, Jonah did not want to go to Nineveh. The Bible says he went down to Tashua, went down to Joppa, and caught a ship going down to Tashua. He went down into the lower part of the ship and went to sleep. Now I want you to note the way I said it. He went down to Joppa, down to Tashua, down into the bottom of the ship; you can't hide from God. When the time has come for you to do what God has assigned you, you can't hide; you've got to do what he said.

Finally, the Lord caught up with Jonah, and he went a little farther down than that. He went down into the sea, down into the belly of a whale, and some of you are there right now today. What you are going through right now is nothing but a physical hell. He carried Jonah down there, and Jonah said he was in hell or in the belly of hell for three days, and he cried out of hell.

Now, when God brings you up, he brings you up. Well, he brought Jonah up out of the sea, brought him up out of the whale, brought him up out of Tashua, brought him up out of Joppa. And when Jonah came out, he was willing to go the full measure.

Joshua had to go the full measure when he fought the battle of Jericho. You see, sometimes going the full measure means nothing more than being willing to do what God says. And you know that's a hard job for some of us, because we don't want to obey God. But to go the full measure, you've got to do what he says.

Well, to start off with, Joshua had a large number of folks, and sometimes we think the victory lies in the majority. But I want to tell you if you're living for Jesus—you and Jesus—you are the majority. You don't need anybody else, because he's God all by himself. He told Joshua when the time came to go to battle; you see, sometimes God wants to test you. I know you think you're ready and you think you can fight the battle. And that's what's wrong with some of us. We get in ourselves, and we get in zeal, and we think we are a little more capable of making it than we are. You know how you get lifted in yourself and you testify, "I'm going to live holy anyhow, and I don't care what you do, what you say, I'm going to make it anyhow."

But let me tell you something: every one of them is a test for you. Every time you say you are going to make it, the devil says,

41

"I'll see. I'll see if you make it." Listen here, he said take them down by the water brook; I know you got a big gang, there's a whole lot of them, but some of them are not worth the salt in their body. He said take them down to the water brook and test them out. Everyone who goes down there and sticks his head down and drinks water without watching, he said put him on your left hand, and every one of them who goes down there and dips his hand, gets some water in it, and drinks and watches at the same time, put him on your right hand.

When the time came to go to battle, Joshua said, "Lord, I don't have but a few folks; how am I going to win the battle?" It's like that in the church today. Whenever it's time for spiritual battle, there are only a few folks. Whenever it's time to battle through prayer, there are only a few people fasting and attending prayer meetings. But God told Joshua, "All you've got to do is follow me. I got the plan. I got the victory and I'm just going to give you the city."

When you're a child of God, you don't have to fight the battle; he'll give you your battle. You don't have to fight for yourself. He'll fight for you. God, you help me here; that's why so many of us were losing the battles, because we're trying to fight them by ourselves, we're trying to fight them with our fleshly warfare, with our worldly guns. But I want to tell you this is a spiritual warfare, and we wrestle not against flesh and blood but against principalities, against spiritual weakness in high places, and it takes the power, the power of the almighty God, to fight the battle.

God told Joshua, "Get your trumpets of rams, forget your singers, forget your shouters, all I want you to do is march, one time, two times, three times, four times, five times, six times, seven times, around the wall." They obeyed God, and the wall came tumbling down. They went the full measure.

Elisha went the full measure. He had to meet Ahab and Jezebel. He met 450 prophets on Mount Carmel. But God gave him the battle, God who answers by fire, and God works where no man can hinder. God, who's a mighty God! God, who's a great God! God, who is a good God! Elisha told the people let us let the

God that answers by fire be God. If your God answers, I'll serve your God. If my God answers, you'll serve my God. And I want to try your God. I want to try him, see who is your God. I want you to tell me, will he answer prayers? Will he hear you when you call him? Will your God help you in the times of trouble? Will your God heal your body when you get sick? Will your God?

Let me tell you about Elisha. That man got out of there; he caught all that fire from heaven. Got lifted up in himself and got scared too. Sometimes all because you win one battle, you think you're somebody. And he slipped from over there, running from Jezebel, because he told him by this time tomorrow, I'm going to make your life as one of the prophets that you slayed on Mt. Carmel. Sometimes the devil will threaten your life if you stand for God. He'll threaten to kill you with all kinds of sickness. He'll threaten you with high blood pressure, and he'll threaten you with cancer.

I am so glad I serve a God who's able to deliver me. That little man, that old man, ran and hid from that woman, but God followed him, and when he sat down he said, "God, I'm by myself. All the prophets are dead, there is nobody left to stand for God but me." But I heard God when he said I have 7,000 who haven't bowed the Baal or kissed him. He had to get up, he had to get up. He had to come out of the cave. He had to come out of hiding, because that's what he was doing; some of you have gotten discouraged and gone into hiding. You are not going to do this and you are not going to do that. You are not going to work with this and you are not going to work with that. But if God is in your life, you've got to come out of your cave, you've got to quit hiding. God wants you to go the full measure.

Now, man must respond to the revelation of Jesus Christ. I have some more: Esther, who went the full measure for the children of Israel, decided, "I'm going in to see the king. I know, I'm not supposed to go. I know, I don't have no business going in there, but Malachi, you go tell them that tomorrow I'm coming to the palace, and if he don't want me, he can go ahead on and kill me. But I am going anyhow." Every one of you ought to make up your mind: I'm going the full measure and be like Esther: if I perish, I'm going to see the king.

The text tells the story of a man who thought he had it made; he went out there to earn his living by farming and made real good profits. He made pretty good. He said, "I'll tell you what I'm going to do. I'm going to tear these barns down. I'm going to build me some more because I've done real good. I've got good money. I can retire. I don't have to work no more. I can sit down and take it easy."

And you probably know some folks who are just like that. They're on their way to hell but taking it easy. They are employed by the devil, but they're taking it easy. They think they've got it made, but let me tell you, the very night after he built his barn and harvested his crops, God stepped out and said, "Oh thou fool, your soul is required of thee this night, and who shall these things be, which thou possess?"

I must tell you, you may think you have it made in this material world, because you are driving a brand new car and living in luxury; you wear your diamonds, you wear your gold, your silver, your designer clothes, and all your styles, but one day you have to die and leave every bit of it behind. You have to go to God and give an account of every deed that's done on your body. You have to stand before the judgment.

This farmer thought he had gone the full measure. When God called him, he wasn't ready. Jesus struck the parable and said what shall it profit a man to gain the whole world and lose his own soul, or what will you give in exchange for your soul if you want to make it in? You better go the full measure. Jesus in salvation went the full measure. I heard him when he said, "Prepare me a body." I know he lost and man sinned. He was put out of paradise. A flaming sword was put at the entrance of the garden. You couldn't go in the east, you couldn't go in the west, you couldn't go in the north, and you couldn't go in the south. But I'm glad God so loved the world that he gave his only begotten son that whosoever believeth in him should not perish. Jesus went the full measure in redemption; he came down here.

I heard the songwriter when he said, "Living he loved me, dying he saved me, buried he carried my sins far away, rising he justified me, freed me forever, one day he's coming back. What a glorious day!" He came in this world born of a woman. Conceived by the Holy Ghost, lived here, suffered at Mt. Calvary; he did not spare his own life, but he gave it up in the fullness of time. God sent forth his own son, born of a woman, made in the flesh, to redeem man from the curse of the law.

I heard the writer say that he came treading the winepress alone. Daniel said he saw him as a stone hewed out of the mountain. Ezekiel said he saw him as a wheel in the middle of a wheel. Isaiah said he was a Rose of Sharon, he was the prince of peace. He came and lived thirty-three years. There was no sin or guilt found in his mouth. But I heard Isaiah say surely he was wounded for our transgressions, he was bruised for our iniquity, and with his stripes we are healed. Yes, he died. He died in my place: full measure. He died for my sins: full measure. He died for your sins. He died. He died that you might live. He died that you might be free.

But early Sunday morning, he got up out of the grave. I heard him when he said, "Oh grave where is your victory? Oh death where is your sting?" Aren't you glad that he went the full measure? Aren't you glad he went all the way?

Now you have to go the full measure. Paul said, "Oh, that I might know him in the power of his resurrection; that I may be made comfortable unto his death. Oh, that I might know him in the excellence of his knowledge." You've got to go the full measure. You can't quit half way. You can't get tired and stop. You can't get discouraged and quit. You can't let anybody drive you away. You can't let anybody turn you away. If you know the Lord saved your soul, tell the world, "I'm going all the way."

Are you going all the way? Are you going the full measure? Tell the Lord that you are going the full measure. I decided I'm going all the way. I know there are tests. I know there are trials. I know there are heartaches. I know there are burdens. I know there are misunderstandings. I know there are going to be some ups and downs, but I am going the full measure. I am going! The devil is going to try to stop me, but I am going. It may be through your husband, through your children, through your neighbor, through your job, through temptations of temporal things, but I am going.

You don't have to go alone. All you have to do is tell the Lord, "Walk with me. While I'm on this tedious journey, Lord, I want you to walk with me." Remember, he said if you'll go, I'll go with you; therefore, stay on the battlefield. The saints used to sing the song: "I come out here to live right till I die." The songwriter said, "I have decided to walk with Jesus, no turning back, no turning back."

Go the full measure!

CHAPTER 8

Leading with Integrity
Responding to God's Call

The word "respond" means to answer or reply; it means to act when prompted by something or someone. In our case, this someone is God. All of us who are Christians can rejoice in the fact that we have been called from sin unto salvation, from darkness into the light, from death unto life eternal, from condemnation to justification. We have been called out and set apart, and by this we change our way of living.

However, the call for those who lead the church, the body of Christ, the ones who specifically are mentioned in Ephesians 4:11 (the apostles, prophets, evangelists, pastors, and teachers), was given to the church for the edifying of the body of Christ. It is indeed, to us, that the focus is on today. The call is one that indeed can only be given by God, to stand where I'm standing now or to sit where these other leaders are sitting. It is not by the choice of individuals, but by a divine calling. You don't chose to stand here.

With the call to lead comes many great responsibilities. Henry T. Blackaby said, "Be careful to preach faithfully the Word of God; pray earnestly for each of the members, and especially to seek the assistance of the Holy Spirit as you pray; love people deeply as you would your Lord; seek earnestly the fruit of the spirit, and function always with a deep sense of stewardship of the people of God, whom He purchased with His own blood and loves as His treasured possession."

But my focus is that we as leaders must respond to God's call with a life that reflects his image. I believe that leaders are called to preach and lead people into this faith not only by the words of the gospel alone but also by the integrity of their lives.

I want quickly to view Paul's writing to Timothy; Paul gave Timothy not his calling but instructions on how to respond to God's call.

The key verse in 1 Timothy is 3:15: "You will know how people ought to conduct themselves in God's household, which is the church of the living God." Realizing that behavior is based upon belief, Paul stressed sound doctrine.

First and second Timothy and Titus are the three Pastoral Epistles, written to ministers in charge of important churches instead of to the churches themselves. Both Timothy and Titus were given explicit directions for shepherding the sheep and for guarding the churches after Paul was called "home," as he knew he soon would be (2 Timothy 4:7-8).

Timothy had been entrusted with the government and supervision of Ephesus, and Titus of the church at Crete. How inadequate both of theses young men felt.

Because Timothy was a young man, we may expect to find in Paul's writings to him valuable suggestions for other young men who are living the Christian life, and we are not disappointed in this expectation, but we also find helpful suggestions for those who are older in years.

In this day of modern education, it is well to offer each other a commendation of the faith of our forefathers and to warn each other against what is falsely called "knowledge". It is well to encourage each other to "fight the good fight, holding on to faith and a good conscience" And who can hear Paul's words to this young associate without hearing him say across the years to our own selves, "Whatever it costs, keep yourself pure"
(2Timothy5:22).

It was a real honor for the young Timothy to enjoy the friendship of the apostle Paul. He was one of Paul's own converts, and Paul calls him "my son whom I love, who is faithful in the

Lord" (1 Corinthians 4:17). During the impressionable days of Timothy's boyhood, while Paul was visiting Lystra, the people first tried to worship the apostle and then sought to take his life. Timothy had listened to the gospel preached by Paul. He saw him heal the cripple, heard him as he appealed to the multitude, and then saw him stoned and left for dead. But the next day, Paul rose and came again into the city. Among the most enthusiastic converts of that city were Eunice and her son Timothy.

When Paul came back to Lystra on his second missionary journey, he took Timothy along as his companion. What a wonderful thing for so young a man! After long years of training under this mighty man of God, Timothy was left in charge of the important church at Ephesus. This brought the timid young man face-to-face with serious problems. Think of this inexperienced young fellow being left in that big church to take the place of its founder, Paul!

How unworthy he must have felt. He leaned on the apostle for advice and direction.

While Timothy was acting as pastor in Ephesus, Paul wrote his two letters to him, as letters of instruction and guidance indeed to Timothy, but also as a handbook for Christian pastors through the centuries. Paul instructed Timothy to deal severely with false teachers, to direct public worship, to choose church officers, and to work with all classes found in the church. But most important of all, he told him to lead a life that would be an example to all. (Sometimes preachers and leaders act like we forget that our lives are supposed to be an example of the Christ we preach.) Timothy had a hard task.

Paul had won a vast multitude to Christ during his stay in Ephesus. In the succeeding years, the number of converts increased tremendously. Within the next fifty years, so many of the non-Christians turned to Christ that their idolatrous temples were almost forsaken.

One of the things to remember about this time of the early church is that there were no church buildings. Groups of Christians met in homes. No churches were built until about 200 years after Paul's time, after Constantine the Great put an end to the persecution of Christians. This meant that there were hundreds of small congregations, each with its own leader or pastor.

These pastors were called "elders" (Acts 20:17). In the letters to Timothy, they are called "overseers" (1 Timothy 3:1; "bishop" in the King James Version). Timothy's work was with these various pastors. Remember, there were no seminaries to prepare leaders. Paul had to train his own men. But in spite of no buildings and no theological seminaries, and also in spite of continued persecution, the church grew by leaps and bounds.

Warning Against False Teaching (1 Timothy

Paul calls Timothy his "true son in the faith" (1 Timothy1:2). It is clear that the boy was led to Christ by Paul. He was an example of one accepting Christ as a child, because he had been brought up in a home in which the scriptures were taught. This is the kind of Christian experience we need to emphasize today as not only possible but that which should be the normal experience.

There has never been a day when the church has been free from false teachers who present new and strange doctrines. They are hard to combat, because they base their teachings on parts of God's Word; they do not "correctly handle the word of truth" (2 Timothy 2:15) and interpret it as a whole. What the church needs today is instruction in the vital truths. In contrast with the teaching of the law and "myths and endless genealogies" (1 Timothy 1:4), Paul puts "the glorious gospel of the blessed God" (1:11). Therefore in response to God's call Timothy must safeguard against any other doctrine. Don't mix fables and legends with the gospel.

Paul warns Timothy to hold "faith and a good conscience" (1 Timothy 1:19) because these traits save people from spiritual shipwreck. It is an awesome sight to see a ship loosened from her mooring and plunging into the ocean. But it is a solemn sight too, considering the many storms she is likely to meet. If this is true of a ship, how much more so of a Christian starting out on the voyage of life?

Paul speaks plainly of some who, having put away faith and a good conscience, have caused spiritual shipwreck and are wrecked for two worlds. And we must pay heed to his warnings.

Even in the first-century church, Paul was called upon to warn his young coworker Timothy against false teaching, which is much like the false doctrine of the twentieth century. Paul had warned them when he left Ephesus seven years before that "savage wolves" would ravage the flock. (Acts 20:29-30). Now they were there in full force and presented young Timothy with his worst problem.

Paul's charge to Timothy included more than soundness in doctrine. He wanted soundness in life. Paul realized that a person can believe the Word of God completely and yet live a life far from its truth. It is sad when one's life and one's belief are poles apart!

In this letter, Paul says that the best way of fighting error is with a life that measures up to the standards set down in God's Word. Remember, many of us are the only Bibles others ever read. Christians have to live better than other people in this world if their testimony is to count. We either commend Christ to others by our lives or we drive them away from him. How often have we heard, "Well, if that's what Christianity does for a person, I don't want any of it!"

Paul wants Timothy to live a life that will vindicate the truth he preaches. He challenges him to be a good soldier of Jesus Christ. We must remember that we will not fight very hard for a truth we do not live. As with Timothy, so it is with us. What Timothy will preach will be empowered and made mighty by what Timothy is.

Timothy is charged to "fight the good warfare" (1 Timothy 1:18). This presents the thoughts of a battle's campaign and all the responsibilities of the officer in command.

Paul humbly declares, "Here is a trustworthy saying that deserves full acceptance; Christ Jesus came into the world to save sinners, of whom I am the worst" (1:15).

Here we catch a glimpse of the man who probably did more for Christ than any other throughout the ages since the world began, bowed to his knees with the feeling of his own unworthiness. Although Paul was once a blasphemer, now God in his grace had appointed him an apostle; although he had persecuted Christ, now he could proclaim his love. The closer we get to the heart of Christ, the more we realize our own unworthiness. When we fail to get closer to the heart of God, we fail to see our own unworthiness. And that's why as preachers we sometimes exalt ourselves higher than we ought to. We get caught up in the glamour of ministry, and then we call it our ministry and exalt the ministry above the Christ of the ministry.

A singer may think he has a very good voice, but let him compare himself with Caruso, the great Italian operatic tenor, and he will feel as if he should never sing again. The reason many people today do not have a sense of sin is that they are not near to Christ. But just to stand in Christ's presence is enough to make us feel condemned. Paul did not realize how sinful he was until he was brought face to face with his Lord and Savior. He felt his miraculous conversion was intended to be an example of how God can save and use the worse of sinners.

Directions for the Church (1 Timothy 2:1-3)

The church has a great calling. We are not only called upon to plead with people to turn to God but also to plead with God the cause of people. Paul says, "I urge, then, first of all, that requests, prayers, intercession, and thanksgiving be made for everyone, for kings and all those in authority" (1 Timothy 2:1-2). Yes, he tells us to pray for rulers. It is well to remember that Nero was the emperor of Rome at this time. Under this wicked despot, Paul was imprisoned and soon would be beheaded. This proves to us that we must pray for bad rulers as well as good, "that we may live peaceful and quiet lives in all godliness and holiness".

Remember when we pray that God "wants all men to be saved and to come to come to a knowledge of the truth. For there is one God and one mediator between God and men, the man Christ Jesus" (1 Timothy 2:4-5). Paul makes it clear that when we pray for someone we can go straight to God for that person. We need no saint or virgin to approach near to God, only the One who gave himself a ransom for all. Our blessed Lord himself stands in God's presence, pleading for us.

Do you remember the legend of Aeschylus, who was condemned by the Athenians and was just about to be executed? His brother Amyntas, the brave warrior who had just gained a victory for Athens, came into the court. Without a word he held up the bleeding stub of his arm, which had been severed in battle. As the judges looked upon the wound, they said, "For the sake of Amyntas, Aeschylus is counted innocent and set free!"

When we look to heaven and remember that God has condemned us because of our sin, we could despair. But we see Jesus sitting at the right hand of the throne on high, holding up his nail-printed hands, and presenting his pierced feet and wounded side, pleading for you and I.

Finally, let all who pray be clean in conduct and pure in character (1 Timothy 2:8-10). Let us lift "holy hands" when we pray. That means that we should not fill our lives with worthless pleasures or needless things that absorb, but as John said, "Come to the Lord with a heart that is cleansed" (1 John 1:9).

Church Leadership

When we think of church officers, we immediately think of the "official church board." Paul tells us the kind of people who really ought to be on the church board. If the church shall fulfill her mission of proclaiming the gospel and praying for all, then she must be governed properly and know the real reason for her existence. Paul describes two officers to direct the church: bishops and deacons. He outlines the requirement for both groups.

We find as we look at this that the pastor must be a man of blameless character, "husband of but one wife," not quarrelsome, not greedy for money. He must be a skillful teacher, and one who makes his own children obey. He must have a good reputation in his community (1 Timothy 3:2-7). It is important that the church have the right leadership. Good pastors lead a church forward. The hour is too late to be monkey footing around; the church needs good and faithful leaders today.

Deacons must have the same moral qualifications as elder or pastors. This office is not inferior, but different. The two offices were to be complementary to each other. A deacon must be carefully chosen.

Paul shows us the need of Christian conduct. Church manners are a lost art in most places today. It makes a great deal of difference how we behave. Behavior reveals character. It is not "*do*-havior" but "*be*-havior" that counts. What we *are* speaks so loudly that people often cannot hear what we say.

The Church

Paul gives a beautiful description of the church and states her purpose. He tells you how Christians "ought to conduct themselves in God's household, which is the church of the living God, the pillar and foundation of the truth" (1 Timothy 3:15). The church upholds all truth in the sight of people. She is the only earthly institution to which Christ committed the preaching of the gospel.

Directions for the Pastor (1 Timothy 4:2-6)

Picture the young pastor Timothy awed by his instructor, the fifty-year-old apostle Paul, as he says, "In later times some will abandon the faith," giving themselves up to spiritualism and all of its teachings. They will tell you if you would be holy, you must not marry, neither should you eat certain kinds of food. But let us not put a ban on that which God has given for our good. Turn a deaf ear to foolish *"isms"* filled with "do this" and "don't do that." People are always trying to find what they can "do" to inherit eternal life (see 4:2-5). But Paul goes on to say, "If you point these things out to the brothers, you will be a good minister of Christ Jesus" (4:6).

Lead a godly life because "godliness has value" (4-8). True religion is an appeal to common sense. God says it pays. In one way, Christianity is a business. It takes us to get out our account books, to study the current prices, to consider the possibilities of profit and loss, and to decide, "What good is it for a man to gain the whole world, and yet forfeit his soul?" (Mark 8:36). Paul, after taking account, found that what he had counted as "gain" was "loss."

Does it pay to invest in the Christian life? Does it pay from the standpoint of life right now? God says it does. Christ says, "Seek first his kingdom and his righteousness, and all these things will be given to you as well" (Matthew 6:33).

A noted Puritan once said that God had only one Son, and he made him a minister.

Paul says to the young minister and to those of you who may be ministers, "Don't think entirely in terms of the physical, how you can please your body." Everyone is thinking in terms of having fun by doing things. The body must be fed, clothed, and pleased. "Physical training is of some value," says Paul, "but godliness has value for all things, holding promise for both the present life and the life to come" (1 Timothy 4:8). Start living for eternity.

"Set an example for the believers in speech, in life, in love, in faith, and in purity" (4:12). Carry conviction and command respect. In order to do this, give much attention to your reading, preaching, and teaching. The best way to combat any error is by reiterating the simple gospel truth. The Bible itself will do the job, if only you will give it a chance. "Give yourself wholly to the Scriptures" (4:15). If a man is to succeed in the ministry, he must pour all his strength into it.

It demands the whole person, the whole time. Godliness does not starve real living. You will not become a sissy if you are good. Godliness is not "goody-ness." The way a minister treats his flock is of vital importance. He must deal wisely and fairly with each one. Widows must be cared for. Elders must be honored and supported, but they must also be reproved, even in public, if they are found guilty, so that others may be warned.

In other words, sin can never get by in the church, no matter who is guilty of that sin.

Paul even remembers the Christian slaves. They must be taught. Those who serve unbelieving masters are to let their service be a testimony to these unbelievers. Those who serve Christians should not take advantage because of their spiritual relation. Love should make us serve the better. "Fight the good fight" (1 Timothy 6:12). Christ makes his appeal to the heroic in a man or woman.

The Christian's life is not a thing to be entered into lightly. We will not be carried into heaven on flowery beds of ease. We must fight if we would be conquerors. But it is a "good fight."

If we can't follow Paul's instructions, then come on and follow the life and the instruction of Jesus:

"Go to Calvary."

CHAPTER 9

Unity in Ministry

The word "unity" is a small but powerful word. It is a word that needs to ring out among the Christian church. It is a biblical fact that God intended for unity to be an integral part of the church. It is that seemingly missing element that keep churches ingrown and separated by denominations, personalities, race, and egos. When we as church leaders demand the unity of the Body of Christ, it will have a Pentecost effect on the city, not just our local churches. For too long we have selfishly settled for Pentecost experiences within the walls of our own churches, never taking notice that in Acts 2:1, what happened in the Upper Room (the church) was not localized to the Upper Room alone. According to the Bible, the spirit that filled the Upper Room was experienced by the whole city through Peter's preaching. It is worth noting that before the city was affected, unity was in the Upper Room. So therefore, we can see the effects of unity by following the earlier church in the book of Acts.

The word "unity" is defined as oneness, harmony, and agreement. Unity again was apparent on the day of Pentecost, when the believers were all in one accord in one place. Now recall with me the later scene of Pentecost when the Parathions, Medes, Elamites, the dwellers in Mesopotamia, Judea, Cappadocia, Pontus, Asia, Phrygia, Pamphylia, Egypt, parts of Libya, Cyrene, strangers of Rome, Jews and proselytes, Cretes, and Arabians were all amazed, according to Acts 2:7, at the fact that they all heard, in their own native language, the wonderful Word of God, which tells us that the church is a unity in diversity, a fellowship of faith, hope, and love that binds believers together. It was necessary that I list all of the names to show that there was indeed unity in spite of the differences of languages and nationalities; there was unity in the ministry that went forth.

The Christian church is unified in its message, meaning it has one message for all races, ages, and cultures. It is the message of the cross, the gospel of Jesus Christ. Although we are together with our doctrine, we are divided by many walls. We find ourselves standing off from each other. Every ministry has become an island of its own, seeming to say we are able to stand alone as individual bodies of Christ. This is what Paul cautions us on in Romans 12:3-8: "For I say, through the grace given to me, to everyone who is among you, not to think of himself more highly than he ought to think, but to think soberly, as God has dealt to each one a measure of faith. For as we have many members in one body, but all members do not have the same function, so we being many are one body in Christ, and individually members of one another. Having then gifts differing according to the grace that is given to us. Whether prophecy, and let us prophesy according to the proportion of faith. Or ministry, let us wait on our ministering, or he that teacheth, on teaching; or he that exhorteth, on exhortation; he that giveth, let him do it with simplicity; he that ruleth, with diligence; he that showeth mercy, with cheerfulness."

In these verses Paul lets us know, first of all, that we should never think of ourselves or our individual ministries more highly than we ought to think. Rather, we are to think clearly, understanding the measure of faith that God deals out as gifts in a certain measure. This level of spiritual gifts he calls "the measure of faith." We all should realize that others have their share as well as we. Therefore, it will not become us to lift up ourselves and our ministries and to despise others as if we are the only ones with favor in heaven.

Then, Paul goes on and tells us that in spite of the fact that we are many, we are in one body, the body of Christ; each member has its respective place and work assigned to it for the good of the whole body, and our individual ministries complement each other.

Paul goes on to tell us that although we have different gifts, they all edify one body. There is one body of Christ; therefore, no preacher or ministry is an island by itself. We must embrace each other with this biblical understanding. It is the only way to have unity in ministry.

The apostle Paul speaks to us again in Ephesians 4:1-6, where he requests that we walk worthy of the vocation wherewith we are called, having the attitude of lowliness, and meekness, with longsuffering, forbearing one another in love, doing our best to keep the unity of the spirit in the bond of peace. Peace is a bond. Again, there is one body and one spirit, even as we are called in one hope of our calling. There is one Lord, one faith, one baptism, one God, and one Father who owns all true members of the church for his children. He is above all, which means he has dominion over all creatures, especially his one church. He is in us all by the indwelling of his spirit in each believer. Therefore we should acknowledge that no preacher or ministry has a monopoly on what we do for the Kingdom of God. Paul tells us in Philippians 2:13, "For it is God which worketh in us both to will and to do of His good pleasure." All of our working, and all of our accomplishments, depends upon his working in us.

The Bible tells us that where there is unity there is strength, and until there is unity in ministry, our city, our state, our country, and this world will never know the strength of the church. Therefore, for the sake of this crooked and perverse society, let us commit to have unity in ministry and bring about a change that can only be credited to God.

CHAPTER 10

Working Before Harvest Time
Matthew 20:1-7

I would like to talk about a portion of the parable of the laborers, perhaps in a different perspective than we usually look at it. Usually, when we look at this parable, we focus on the laborers, who had worked all day long, bearing the heat of the day, disagreeing with the householder who paid those who had only worked for one hour the same amount as those who worked all day long. We find joy in the fact that Jesus is not going to pay us for the time we are in his vineyard but for the fact that we came into the vineyard and worked diligently.

I only want to talk about laborers in the vineyard, as well as the vineyard itself, and the harvest time for the ripe things of the vineyard. Notice I said the ripe things of the vineyard, because at harvest time, not everything in the vineyard will come out. Now I want you to think spiritually with me here. We're going to talk about two different vineyards. One is cultivated land, the dirt fields with vegetation growing in them. The other is the spiritual vineyard, where we are talking about the work of the Lord. Not everything in the vineyard is good, and even at harvest time, not everything in the vineyard is ripe. Have you ever gone out when strawberries were supposed to be ripe, and when you started picking them, you found there were many that weren't ripe? Well, undoubtedly you only picked those that were ripe. You only brought out of the field those that were good, those ready for harvesting. Well, *Webster's* says a vineyard is "land devoted to cultivating grapevines." The second definition in *Webster's* is "a field of activity of spiritual labor."

The first mention of the vineyard is in Genesis 9:20. It talks about when Noah began farming and planted a vineyard. Jesus used the vineyard in many of his parables. In Matthew 9:17, you will find the parable of the cloth and the wine skins. Also, in Matthew 21:28 you will find the parable of the two sons who were sent out to work in the vineyard by their father; when asked to go, one said he would go and didn't go (that sounds like church people), and the other said he wouldn't go and later repented and went. Then, over in Luke 13:6-9, you will find the parable of the fig tree planted in the midst of the vineyard.

There is a lot to say about the vineyard. Here in Matthew 20, we're told of the householder who went out to hire laborers because it was harvesting time. There are many reasons why, throughout the day, he kept on calling in those he found standing idle in the marketplace. It wasn't solely because he felt they needed work. The grape harvest ripened toward the end of September, and then close behind this time was the rainy season. If the grapes weren't gathered in before the rain broke, then the harvest would be ruined. So the owner of the vineyard hired anyone he could get to work, even those who only worked for one hour. They were welcome to work and gather in as many grapes as they could.

Other than gathering in the harvest, there were other jobs in the vineyard; there was the job of the vine dresser, who was hired to care for the vines and pruned them yearly. There was the job of hedging or fencing the vineyard to protect it from wild animals. Then there was the job of the vineyard guard. They would erect a tower and place a guard in it to protect the vines against robbers. So as you can see, there were many things to do in the cultivated land vineyard.

There are many things to do in the spiritual vineyard of the Lord, just like the vineyard of cultivated land. In fact, there is a whole lot more work to do in the Lord's vineyard. Jesus said himself in Matthew 9:37-38, "The harvest truly is plenteous, but the laborers are few. Pray ye therefore the Lord of the harvest, that he will send forth laborers into his harvest."

Now, here Jesus gives a second picture of mankind. The first is sad ("the multitude is like a ravaged flock"), but this is glad: "The multitude is like a harvest field waiting for the reaper." There are two natures in man, divided by a cleft in the very will. Man is perverse, but he can still say with truth (as Peter said with truth, despite his failures), "Lord, thou knowest all things and thou knowest that I love thee."

So here, Jesus saw men ready to respond to the gospel and granted enough reapers. If he had enough reapers, and that being men and women of Christian speech and of a Christian heart, many of the multitude could be won for God. They should, because men are God's field, made for life with him. When God created us, he created us for himself. God didn't create any man for hell, since he is the Lord of the harvest. But without reapers, the harvest maybe lost.

Remember, I told you that harvest time for the grapes was in September, but they had to hurry up and gather in the harvest because the rainy season closely followed. If they didn't get the grapes in before the rains came, then the harvest would be lost. Well, it's the same thing with the Lord's vineyard. We Christians are laborers, we are reapers, and we must work and draw men and women into the Lord's vineyard before harvest time, because at harvest time, it's too late to go out and try to compel men and women to Christ. It's too late. We can't wait until the harvest time of the Lord to start working. You can't go to heaven by yourself.

So here in these verses, Jesus yearned for more men of his mind to help him. He knew that he must delegate the work. Why? Because we are his workmanship. I want you to know that every child of God reading this today has been delegated to us. If you don't want the job, then you don't want to be a Christian.

We see in these verses the beginning of an ordained ministry and an unordained ministry. What kind of ministry? Well, men and women who see life as God's field, men and women who work with abounding hope because the harvest truly is plenteous, versus men and women who live only for their fellow man, and God, in self-forgetting love.

Let me deal with self-forgetting love. You can't really learn how to love other people until you forget about loving yourself. There are so many Christians (not just here, but everywhere you go) who are hung up on themselves. You can't help anybody loving yourself to death. But we've got to get to the point and say, like Paul said, "I am less than the least." Then, you can help somebody."

Verses 37 and 38 express the cruciality of prayer. Jesus says, "Pray ye therefore one for another." Now understand that this prayer should not be the substitute for the labor. Many times we say if we pray for the unsaved, that's enough. But no, we've got to labor to gather in the lost souls. Honey, you can pray all you want to, but those folks out there don't even know you're praying for them.

But when you go face to face and say, "Brother, I love you, and you might not like what I have to tell you, you may not even want to hear it. But I must tell you that Jesus hung, bled, suffered, and died for your sins and mine, and you don't have to live like this. You can live adjacent from the world."

Now, don't get confused. I didn't say you don't have to pray, because the disciples were to be reapers as well as praying men; the work will not be done without prayer. Now let me turn it around and let you know there is no need in going out there if you haven't prayed first. You have got to have a prayer life. The work cannot be done without prayer. Intercession has mighty power: it is God's channel for raising up leaders in the Christian cause. Now this saying of Christ has wide implications. For example, the world needs fewer men to invent things and manipulate things and far more men to cultivate the field of mankind and reap the harvest of the soul.

This necessary change of emphasis has profound meaning for economics and education, as well as for mission, field, and church. Now listen to this: Oliver Goldsmith dedicated his poem "The Traveler" to his brother, who became a Christian, and he complimented his brother on entering a real harvest field. He told him, "You have left the field of ambition where the laborers are many, and the harvest is not worth carrying away." Folks in the world, those who are unsaved, you are a part of a harvest, but you're not worth being carried away. If you find yourself in the wrong harvest, you better cross over. I told you that not everything in the physical field at harvest time was worth coming out of the field; not everything is ripe at harvest time.

When Christ comes back, he's coming to pull out of the field all his laborers who are ripe in heart, all who are true laborers of Christ, and all who are saved. Jesus is coming back to pull us out and take us from earth to glory. But he's going to leave everybody who is not saved, leave them planted in the earth, because he only wants the wheat out of the field. The tare he doesn't need.

If you're a Christian, you are considered wheat, but if you're unsaved, you are considered tare. We need not try to point out who's wheat and who's tare, because the scriptures already told us that we can't tell the difference. Man has never been able to rightly separate all of the wheat. Man did the best he could do to separate the tare out of the wheat, because he didn't need the tare mixed with the wheat; the wheat was food and it was sold, and it was a trade item. But the tare was a poisonous grass that looked like wheat. Poisonous grass in the churchfolks who try to kill every program they're not in charge of—poisonous grass; folks who try to kill the pastor and ministers of the church with vile rumors—poisonous grass; folks who show up on Sunday morning with those haughty spirits, trying to hinder worship service—poisonous grass; folks who show up for choir rehearsal mumbling and grumbling (they have more mouth than the piano has keys)—poisonous grass.

Oh yes, it's sad, but it's true. There is poisonous grass in the church. Now let's go back to the wheat and tare out in the dirt field. Man has always tried to separate the wheat from the tare. So to separate it, man took into consideration that the seeds in the tare were smaller than the seeds in the wheat, which meant the wheat was heavier than the tare. So they would take a winnowing fork and take the tare and the wheat, which was mixed together, and toss it up into the air. The wind would blow the lightweight tare out of the heavy wheat, and the wheat would fall back to the ground. Man, being imperfect, couldn't get all of the tare out of the wheat, so undoubtedly, we know that some tare fell back down with the wheat. But that just goes to show you that when you think you have everything right in the church, you look over there in the corner and see some tare you missed. But I'm so glad that Jesus knows how to perfectly separate the tare from the wheat.

When Jesus comes back, no tare shall mistakenly be called up with the wheat. So everybody, please examine yourself. Are you wheat or are you tare? Understand that wheat can look like tare. Before men you walk like a Christian, you talk like a Christian, you dress like a Christian, you sing in the choir, you usher, you work on the unsaved, you work hard in the church, but are you saved? Well, and if you are saved, then work on the unsaved. Work on those who are lost. Work on those who are in the world. Work the plan of salvation. Work the gospel of Jesus Christ. Work and compel men and women to come to Christ. Work before it's harvest time. Harvest time! Armageddon. Revelation 14:14 tells us about your vision of harvest time:

"Well, I looked and behold, a white cloud, and upon the cloud sat one like the son of man, having on his head a golden crown, and in his hand a sharp sickle." (The Son of God on the cloud.)

"And another angel came out of the temple, crying with a loud voice to him that sat on the cloud, Thrust in thy sickle, and reap; for the time is come for thee to reap; for the harvest of the earth is ripe" (Revelation 14:15).

Now I know it may seem funny that an angel would come from the altar and tell the Son of God what to do. But the Word of God has already told us that no man knows the hour, nor the day, not even the Son.

"And he that sat on the cloud, thrust in his sickle on the earth, and the earth was reaped" (Revelation 14:16).

"And another angel came out of the temple, which is in heaven. He also having a sharp sickle" (Revelation 14:17).

Honey, at harvest time there is going to be some reaping going on.

"And another angel came out from the altar, who had power over fire, and cried with a loud cry to him that had the sharp sickle, saying, "Thrust in thy sharp sickle and gather the clusters of the vine of the earth; for her grapes are fully ripe" (Revelation 14:18).

"And the angel thrust in his sickle into the earth, and gathered the vine of the earth, and cast it into the great winepress of the wrath of God" (Revelation 14:19).

When Noah harvested his grapes and put them in the winepress, the winepress was trodden, and grape juice came out of that winepress. But come on and see what comes out of this winepress of the wrath of God:

"And the winepress was trodden outside the city, and blood came out of the winepress" (Revelation 14:20).

The blood was the blood of the unsaved; the blood of the lost souls; the blood of those who would not believe; the blood of those we failed to reach; the blood of those we turned up our noses at and kept walking; the blood of those we were too clean to touch.

Oh saints of God, can't you see there's work for us to do? We've got to work while it's day. We've got to work before it's harvest time. Listen to what the songwriter has told us to do:

"Throw out the lifeline across the dark wave. There is a brother whom someone should save . . . . Throw out the lifeline with a hand quick and strong. Why do you tarry, why linger so long? Can't you see he is sinking? . . . Throw out the lifeline to danger fraught men, sinking in anguish where you've never been. Winds of temptation and billows of woe will soon hurl them out where the dark waters flow. Soon will the season of rescue be over. Soon will they drift to eternity's shore. Haste, then, my brother, no time for delay, but throw out the lifeline and save them today."

Yes, that's what we've got to do.

Throw out the lifeline, because somebody is drifting away. Somebody is sinking. Somebody is going down for the last time; somebody is on their way to hell. Throw out the lifeline; I don't want the blood of lost souls on my hand, so I'm determined to throw it out, and for your work, for your time, for your ministries through music to lost souls, whatever is right, the owner of the vineyard will pay you.

CHAPTER 11

Preaching with a Problem
2 Corinthians 12:7-10

The preaching of the gospel is the most important occupation any person can be called to do. It ranks as one of the highest stress-level jobs in existence. Medical doctors have concluded that one hour of preaching (Pentecostal style) is equivalent to eight hours of daily labor.

Although it is the most important occupation in the world, preaching is also a highly criticized profession. Anyone who has preached the gospel for any length of time can bear witness that this is a job in which you must endure persecution, envy, strife, jealousy, and stigmatizing. Preachers always seem to be under scrutiny.

With all of these problems, preachers must never back down from what God has called, hired, appointed, and anointed them to do. Although preachers should always be respected and cared for, they should never be the focal point of their own ministry. Instead, the focus should be on souls who are in need of this glorious gospel we are allowed to preach. This is the motivation of preachers: they have a message to deliver straight from their heart to the hearer's very soul.

Despite Resistance and Lack of Time, Preach

Sometimes, the biggest problem preachers have involves speaking to a congregation they know doesn't want to change. So preachers deliver their sermons with a hope the power of the gospel will create a change, even in unexpected places and people. Sometimes it does, as it did in the wicked city of Nineveh, after Jonah delivered a powerful sermon. (The governor on down to the ordinary people repented.) But from that same Bible, we also find that sad story of a preacher named Noah, who preached daily to people who refused to change. Despite not seeing any change, the preacher kept on preaching.

Actually, preachers will always testify that they are preaching with a problem, even though their faithful study of the Word of God, as well as their reading of good books, helps produce rich sermons.

Protestant preachers are not as fortunate as the Roman Catholic, Episcopal, and Lutheran denominations, which have weekly sermons prepared for them. Instead, we must allow the guidance of the Holy Spirit to be paramount in our sermon preparation. Thus, *time* often becomes a problem for some preachers, particularly the bi-vocational ones. We are always preaching with a problem.

Despite Your Past and Physical Problems, Preach

From our text we have this energetic, commanding, masterful man, one of the greatest characters in the Bible and history: the apostle Paul, who became the chief missionary after having been a persecutor of Christ and of Christians.

Paul endeavored enthusiastically to stamp out the Christian faith. In fact, he was standing there when they stoned Deacon Stephen to death. But on the Damascus Road, the persecutor became a believer. (Some of the problems that Paul encountered resulted from his past. You may not know, but some folk will never forget what you used to be. God doesn't consult with your past to determine your future.) In spite of it all, Paul became a great missionary and church builder and undertook three fruitful missionary journeys. In all of his travels, trials, and triumphs, Paul was borne along by one incentive: "to do the will of Him that sent me."

Paul was a heart stirring preacher in spite of his problems. Three of Paul's sermons are preserved for us in the book of Acts, and they serve as models for preachers of all time. He relied upon Old Testament scripture and appealed to historical facts and prophecy. When you ponder his sermon to the Jews at Antioch, and his sermon to the Gentiles at Athens, you can see that Paul was considerate of the people's needs: spiritual, physical, mental, and moral. In the same way, today's preachers should always shoot for the heart and not the feet.

Paul was a gifted writer; of the twenty-seven books that make up the New Testament, he was the author of fourteen of them, if you include the book of Hebrews.

Along with his other problems, Paul's bodily size and appearance may have been against him. Little of stature and partly bald, he also had crooked legs; his eyes were set close together, and he had a hooked nose. But in spite of his physical deformities, Paul lived only to win others to Christ and to make Him known.

Despite Your Thorn in the Flesh, Preach

In our text we read that Paul, like preachers today, had received great revelations. As preachers we must remember that all of our revelation knowledge is a gift from God. Paul was tempted to become conceited in light of his great revelations. To keep that from happening, God sent him a thorn in his flesh. This expression, similar to the Septuagint terminology, "thorn in the side," was a metaphorical description of trouble inflicted by God. It is difficult to know precisely what the apostle had in mind. He also called it a messenger of Satan that brought him torment, but said nothing else. Several things could have been meant by "a thorn in the flesh." First, Paul had a physical ailment, according to Galatians 4:15. He could have had an eye disease or a speech impediment. Second, Paul spoke of continuing opponents in the church. Finally, he pointed to some troubling demonic activity, perhaps some severe temptations.

Despite this uncertainty, Paul's main idea is clear. He asked God three times to remove this thorn from his life, to help him to be more effective in ministry. Yet, God told him that divine grace was sufficient for him. The tense of the expression he used may also be translated as "He has said," indicating that Paul regarded God's statement as more than one simply directed toward his present situation. God wanted Paul to find comfort and security in the grace he had received in Christ, the same thing God desires for all believers.

In fact, in this particular case, God's denial of Paul's request turned out to be for Paul's greater good, because it was for God's greater glory. God told Paul that divine power is made perfect in weakness. Throughout the scripture, God delights in displaying His power in situations where human strength is weak (1 Samuel 14:6-15). When God's people are weak, then God's strength becomes evident.

As a result, Paul determined that he would boast all the more gladly about his weakness. He quit complaining, so that Christ's power might rest on him. The word translated as "rest" (*episkenoo*) may also be translated as "to tabernacle" or "pitch a tent." It is likely that Paul drew upon Old Testament imagery of the glory of God coming upon the tabernacle (Exodus 40:34-38). If so, he learned that taking delight in his thorn actually brought glory in his ministry and preaching. From this understanding of his weakness, Paul concluded that he would delight in his weaknesses rather than harbor resentment about them.

Paul had to suffer imprisonment and continuous exposure to death. (He received thirty-nine lashes five times, was beaten with rods three times, and was shipwrecked three times.) He often suffered from cold and hunger, and his life was endangered by bandits, Jews, and Gentiles. But most of all, Paul made it known that he suffered the most within himself because of the sorry condition of the church.

All of this could be classified as elements of Paul's thorn. Paul said he begged the Lord to take it away. Nevertheless, the Lord kept telling Paul, "My Grace is sufficient for thee" (which means "My favor is all you need"; in other words, "So what if you got problems, as long as I keep blessing you?"). God was telling Paul, "I know you feel weak from troubles, but my power works best in your weakness."

After Paul heard this, he was encouraged and said, "Well, since I know it is all for Christ's good, I am content with my thorn, with my weakness, insults, hardships, persecution, and calamities. For when I am weak, then I am strong."

- When they lie about you, it hurts (yet he's going to bless you), but it makes you stronger; preach!
- When they pull against your vision, it hurts, but it makes you stronger; preach!
-
- When they refuse to support you, it hurts, but it makes you stronger; preach!
- When you're afflicted, it hurts, but it makes you stronger; preach!
- When you're tired, it hurts, but it makes you stronger; preach!
- When you're hurt, it makes you stronger; preach!
- When nobody understands you, it hurts, but it makes you stronger; preach!
- When you feel like throwing in the towel, preach!

When you feel like you are weak, that's a good time to preach, because Paul said that's when you're at your best. That's when you are strongest, when you find yourself preaching with (and in spite of) your problems:

- *Moses had a problem with inadequacy.* He felt like he did not have what it took to be effective. All he had was his walking stick, because he was old, along with his stuttering problem. But God told him, "Take your stick and your stutter and go!"
- *Jonah had a problem of bitterness, fear, and resentment.* He went through hell but discovered that he still had to preach with his problems.
- *The Samaritan woman had a problem of lost dignity and respect.* Yet she had to go back and preach to a city where she had no favor: "Come see a man!"
- *Priscilla's problem was that she lived in a time when it was said that women should be quiet, and Christians were persecuted.* But in spite of her problems, she preached.
- *Paul had problems down in Athens.* They told him he wasn't anything, counted him as nothing but a babbler, but Paul kept on preaching about an unknown God.
- *Hosea had a problem named Gomer, the prostitute.* But he still prophesied to the Israelites.
- *Jesus had his problems, and they called him a devil.* But he still preached about the kingdom of God.
- *Jeremiah summed it all up.* First, he had a problem with his age and felt like he would be despised for his youth. Then he had a problem with God; he was upset because he felt like God didn't hold up his end of the prophecy. Jeremiah was being ridiculed, so he said, "That's it! I've got a problem! No longer will I even mention his name; no longer will I speak in his name. Yet his word is like a burning fire shut up in my bones, and it's making me weary. In spite of my problems I've got to preach, lest I die."

As preachers today, each one of us is compelled to say:

- I've got to tell the sick that there is a balm in Gilead.
- I've got to tell the sinners that the wages of sin is death, but there is an escape from death.
- I've got to tell the backsliders that God is a God of second chances.
- I've got to tell the saints about prosperity and all of their inheritance.

The apostle Paul said, "Woe, woe, woe unto me if I preach not this glorious gospel" (1 Corinthians 9:16). He also declared, "Oh how sweet are the feet of those who preach the gospel" (Romans 10:15, cf Isaiah 52:7).

Paul told his young apprentice Timothy, "I have fought a good fight and I have kept the faith. Now the only thing I see is a crown for me" (2 Timothy 4:7-8). Well, I just want to encourage you to fight on:

- Your steps may be getting slow, but that's all right. Fight on!
- Your voice may not be as strong as it used to be, but that's all right. Fight on!
- You may not be able to do in this season of your life what you did in the other seasons of your life, but that's all right. Fight on!

MOUNT MORIAH COMMUNITY CHURCH
1014 GARNER ROAD, RAL. NC ~ 6PM SUNDAY

There is power in the preach Word!

Bishop Limmie Nathaniel Forbes

In 1959, Pastor Forbes established Faith Temple No. 1 in East Orange, New Jersey, and in 1962, Faith Temple No. 2, now in Capitol Heights, Maryland. In 1978, Bishop Forbes established Faith Temple No. 3 in St. Paul, North Carolina.

As the Presiding Bishop of the Original Free Will Baptist Conference, he spearheaded the construction of the L.N. Forbes Tabernacle in Wilson, North Carolina, which was dedicated in 1975. He now serves as the General Bishop of the Original Free Will Baptist Conference of America, the Vice President of the National Convention of Free Will Baptist of USA, President of the East Orange Clergy Movement and Past President of the Hampton University Ministers Conference.

Dr. Garner C. Taylor & I in Durham, N.C. (2012)

My Favorite Quote from him: "Preaching a bad sermon a long time doesn't make a sermon any better, every preacher must know when to sit down."

Dr. **Gardner Calvin Taylor** (born June 18, 1918) is an American preacher, noted for his eloquence and deep understanding of Christian faith and theology and known as "the dean of American preaching". Taylor was a close friend and mentor to Martin Luther King Jr. and played a prominent role in the religious leadership of the Civil Rights Movement of the 1960s.

Taylor preached the pre-inauguration sermon in January 1993 for the then President-elect Bill Clinton at Metropolitan A.M.E. Church in Washington D.C. Taylor received the Presidential Medal of Freedom on August 9, 2000, awarded by President Bill Clinton.

Gardner Taylor was born in 1918 in Baton Rouge, the grandson of former slaves, and grew up in the segregated South of the early 20th century. He graduated from the Oberlin College School of Theology in 1940, and began a lifetime of preaching and civil rights activism.

Taylor was pastor of the Concord Baptist Church of Christ in Brooklyn, New York for 42 years, before retiring in 1990. During this time he helped to found the Progressive National Baptist Convention with Martin Luther King Jr., providing an important base of support for King's civil rights work.

More than 2,000 of Taylor's sermons are archived, and recordings of many of them are available in collections such as *The Words of Gardner Taylor: 50 years of timeless treasures.*

PREACHING MOMENTS

MIN. ODIS B. ALFORD
DR. ABNER B. ALFORD
DR. AARON B. MCNAIR , SR.
MIN. AARON B. MCNAIR JR.

4 GENERATIONS OF PREACHERS

From top to bottom:
> My Grandfather—Odis B. Alford—Former Pastor in the Church of Christ; Newark, New Jersey
> My Father—Dr. Abner B. Alford—Former Pastor in the Church of Christ; Miami, Florida
> Myself—Pastor Aaron McNair Sr.; Mt. Moriah Church Farmville, N.C. & Mt. Moriah Community Church Raleigh, N.C.; Founder of Life Changing International Fellowship
> My Son—Elder Aaron McNair Jr.; Associate Minister of the Mt. Moriah Churches

COLLEAGUES IN THE PREACHING MINISTRY

Bishop Iona Locke
Abyssina Christ Centered
Ministries
Southfield, MI

Bishop J. Delano Ellis
Founding President of the Joint
College of African American
Pentecostal Bishops & Pastor of
the Pentecostal Church of Christ
Cleveland, OH

Dr. Jasmin W. Sculark A.k.a. Dr. Jazz
Pastor Shiloh Baptist Church
York, PA

Dr. John E. Guns
Senior Pastor of St. Paul
Church of Jacksonville, Inc.
Jacksonville, FL

COLLEAGUES IN THE PREACHING MINISTRY

Pastor Shirley Caesar (Williams)
Mt. Calvary Word of Faith Church
Raleigh, N.C.

Bishop Mark Moore, Sr.
Faith Covenant Church
Decatur, GA

COLLEAGUES IN THE PREACHING MINISTRY

Bishop Elect J. Derrick Johnson
Gospel Tabernacle United Holy Church
Columbus, OH

Dr. James Johnson
Former Pastor of Mt. Zion Pentecostal Church
Washington, DC
Senior Statesman of the United Holy Church of America

Bishop Ralph E. Love, Sr.
Pastor of Holy Trinity United Holy Church
Greenville, NC
President of the Southern District Convocation
2nd Vice President of the National UHCOA

Bishop Kenneth White
Pastor of Linconia Tabernacle Christian Center
Trevose, PA
Vice President of the Northern District Convocation

COLLEAGUES IN THE PREACHING MINISTRY

Dorinda Clarke-Cole
Southfield, MI

Dr. Wayne Thompson
St. Petersburg, FL
Dr.Eugene Gibson
Memphis, TN

Apostle Stephanie Hart
Goldsboro, NC

Apostle Gloria Gaines
Baltimore, MD

Bishop Jesse Jones
Ayden, NC

COLLEAGUES IN THE PREACHING MINISTRY

Elder Christopher Brown
& Elder Harold Hayes

Bishop Patricia Holder
Barbados

Bishop Sinclair Howell
Barbados

Apostle D. Edward Penn
II Hampton, VA, Overseer
Jeremiah Martian

Dr. Clifton E. Buckrham Sr.
Greensboro, NC

Dr. Joel Cliff Gregory
Forth Worth, TX

COLLEAGUES IN THE PREACHING MINISTRY

Pastor Michael Moshokoa
Orange Farm, South Africa

MISSION MINISTRY

COLLEAGUES IN THE PREACHING MINISTRY

Dr. Kenneth Campbell, Dr. Jasmin Scularck, Dr. Jewel London, Dr. Sherry Graham, and Dr. Cynthia Hale.

Dr. Jewel London

Bishop Will Compton

Pastor Val & Jon
Kimble Free Church
Buckinghamshire, England

Peaches Sullivan, Mary Murphy, Crystal Gay, 1st Lady Salome Moshokoa, Letasha Basnight, Pastor Kantoro Stoffel, Pastor Dennis Dube, Apostle Aaron McNair Sr. Pastor Michael Moshokoa, Pastor William Selepe

Bishop Kenneth O. Robinson
National Vice President of United Holy Church of America
Pastor of New Covenant Temple UHC New York, NY
32 years

Tony McIntyre and Apostle Donnie L. McIntyre
Founder & Pastor of Christ Memorial Interdenominational Church
Goldsboro, NC
Spiritual Father to many young preachers

Dr. Joe Samuel & Doris Ratliff
Brentwood Baptist Church
Houston, TX

Martin Luther King III
Activist and Public Speaker

Every preacher needs to surround his/ her self with
a powerful prayer team.

Colossians 1:9-11

New International Version (NIV)

9 For this reason, since the day we heard about you, we have not stopped praying for you. We continually ask God to fill you with the knowledge of his will through all the wisdom and understanding that the Spirit gives,[a] **10** so that you may live a life worthy of the Lord and please him in every way: bearing fruit in every good work, growing in the knowledge of God, **11** being strengthened with all power according to his glorious might so that you may have great endurance and patience

From left to right:
Elder Linda Moore, Apostle A.B. McNair Sr., Elder Radford S. Rogers,
Elder Michael Artis and Elder Mardrecius Edswards.

FAMILY

Courtney, Jaquetta, Aaron Jr., Michelle, and Aaron Sr.

Apostle Aaron & Elect Lady Michelle McNair